THE ONLY SALES GUIDE
YOU'LL EVER NEED

The
ONLY SALES GUIDE
YOU'LL EVER NEED

ANTHONY IANNARINO

PORTFOLIO / PENGUIN

An imprint of Penguin Random House LLC
375 Hudson Street
New York, New York 10014

ISBN 9780735211674 (hardcover)
ISBN 9780735211681 (ebook)

Printed in the United States of America
3   5   7   9   10   8   6   4

Set in Warnock Pro with Neutraface 2
Book design by Daniel Lagin

The *Only Sales Guide You'll Ever Need* is available at a discount when purchased in quantity for sales promotions or corporate use. Special editions, which include personalized covers, excerpts, and corporate imprints, can be created when purchased in large quantities. For more information, please call (212) 572-2232 or e-mail specialmarkets@ penguinrandomhouse.com. Your local bookstore can also assist with discounted bulk purchases using the Penguin Random House corporate Business-to-Business program. For assistance in locating a participating retailer, e-mail B2B@penguinrandomhouse.com.

CONTENTS

CONTENTS

CONTENTS

FOREWORD

THERE IS AN EPIDEMIC OF UNPRECEDENTED PROPORTIONS IN the sales profession today: everyone is looking for the shortcut—the easy fix to producing better sales results now. Sales leaders and individual salespeople are constantly in search of the latest trick, tool, or process, hoping to find the magic bullet. Unfortunately, many currently popular sales authors, bloggers, and supposed experts (some of whom are actually charlatans) are all too happy to offer a continuous stream of appealing, ineffective nonsense that tickles the ears of lazy, desperate sellers who are either afraid or unwilling to do what's necessary to succeed. Sadly, committed, driven sales professionals wanting to hone their craft are also sucked in sometimes.

Enter Anthony Iannarino and *The Only Sales Guide You'll Ever Need*. You won't find many books like this or authors willing to share the hard truth. Instead of telling you what you want to hear and offering yet another "get rich quick" or "lose weight while doubling your carbohydrate intake without exercise" scheme, Anthony pulls back the covers to expose deeper truths about who wins big in sales, why they win, and how they do it.

If you were hoping for a quick fix, I apologize; this isn't the book for you. However, if you are prepared to learn what makes top producers superior to their competition and you are serious about becoming a true sales pro who wins big year after year, congratulations! You've come to the right author and picked up the right book.

In *The Only Sales Guide You'll Ever Need*, Anthony tackles a crucial, central question. And honestly, this really is the only relevant question: Why do a few highly successful salespeople consistently outperform their peers?

I've followed Anthony closely for the past five years and believe he's uniquely positioned and qualified to answer this question. I'm not quite sure when Anthony sleeps. He is a partner and executive in a very successful staffing company, leading its high-performance sales team, and he regularly speaks internationally on a variety of important sales topics. He has somehow found a way to write a sales blog post every single day, for the last couple thousand days, that is read by tens of thousands of people. Yes, Anthony knows sales, salespeople, and sales leadership, and he's bold enough to tell you what you need to know rather than what's popular. He is one of the very few people on the planet whom I turn to for sales wisdom.

This book is built on a critical premise: contrary to what most underperformers claim, sales success is not situational. No, it's not about the market, the product, the company, or the competition. It is all about the seller—the individual.

Furthermore, sales success is not a mystery. In fact, it's far from it. All you need to do is look at top producers across various companies and industries. They exhibit in spades the elements that Anthony writes about! It's not an accident or coincidence; these top sellers own the fact that *they* are the key to their own sales success.

This book is well written and beautifully structured. Part 1 examines the mind-set and behaviors that produce sales results. It is refreshing to read why top performers consistently win before tackling how they do it. The reality is that if you're not willing to look in the mirror and evaluate the elements of the book's part 1, there's no sense jumping into part 2. Embodying mind-set comes first. Once we know the behaviors that lead to success, only then can we turn our attention to skills development. That's true in life, true in relationships, true in sports, true in all areas of business, and most definitely true in sales.

Anthony doesn't hold back the good stuff. The first chapter of *The Only Sales Guide You'll Ever Need* jumps right into the deep end to look at the importance of self-discipline and what he calls "me management." Do not skip ahead or blow through this chapter. Many of the following elements build on the foundational truths in this chapter.

Once you've read through Anthony's master class on mind-set in part 1, you'll tackle skills development in part 2, which is as powerful as it is practical. While the attributes, attitudes, and behaviors taught in part 1 position you to win in sales, the skills revealed in part 2 show you not only how to effectively execute the sales attack but also how to win decisively. Anthony leaves no stone unturned, looking at all the essential elements, ranging from prospecting (opening relationships) to closing (gaining commitments) and everything in between. You'll learn to tell a better story and ask more insightful questions that not only set you apart from your competition but also help move your client toward action. The final chapters will kick you up to another skill level altogether to help you increase your effectiveness in more complex sales.

Anthony makes the strong case that to succeed today, we need to be more than just great salespeople. We must become great businesspeople. He shares valuable tips to increase your business acumen and set you apart in your clients' eyes. He also ensures that you understand the importance of building consensus and how to navigate your dream client's organization—connecting with various stakeholders so you can masterfully quarterback and advance your best opportunities down the field to score.

If you are serious about winning big and winning for the long term in sales, grab your favorite beverage, a highlighter, a pad, and a pen, and turn the page. I guarantee you that *The Only Sales Guide You'll Ever Need* offers exactly what you need to become a top producer.

Enjoy the transformation.

MIKE WEINBERG

President, the New Sales Coach, and author of *Sales Management. Simplified: The Straight Truth about Getting Exceptional Results from Your Sales Team*

THE ONLY SALES GUIDE YOU'LL EVER NEED

INTRODUCTION

I AM AN ACCIDENTAL SALESPERSON.

Right before graduating from high school, I saw the great British hard-rock act Whitesnake perform at Veterans Memorial Auditorium in Columbus, Ohio. Just seventeen years old and wowed by the way women in the audience responded to the lead singer, David Coverdale, I called my older brother, Mike, after the show and told him we had to form a rock-and-roll band. Immediately.

Our little band did well, and within a few years, we were playing the best clubs in Columbus. At age twenty-one, eager for stardom, I headed out to Los Angeles, determined to become a lead singer in a new hard-rock band. But I needed a day job to survive. Since I had already worked in my family's temporary-staffing business as a recruiter, I took a job with a firm that supplied temporary employees to all kinds of companies in and around LA.

After I had been working in the staffing office for a few months, the manager who had hired me was called back to New York City to deal with a family emergency, and I ended up with a new manager—the last thing anyone wants or needs. During the first week, the new manager pretty much ignored me. I was working a light-industrial desk, interviewing candidates for warehouse work, and, with hair down to my waist, I probably wasn't all that interesting to him. I certainly did not look like someone who could help him grow the branch for which he was now responsible.

Then, one day, he approached me and asked, "What do salespeople do?"

Not understanding his question, I gave him a lame answer about calling on companies and winning orders.

Impatiently, he rephrased his question: "What do *our* salespeople do?"

Suddenly, I understood his point. He had come to believe that the three salespeople in our office weren't doing much, and he was correct. I said very little, being unwilling to rat out my coworkers. I couldn't know it at the time, but all three salespeople would be gone within a month.

I am certain my new manager kept me because he recognized that I was a hard worker. Not only was I filling orders, I was also selling and winning accounts, even though I would never have called what I was doing selling.

After firing the entire sales force for their unwillingness to get out and sell, the manager approached me again. This time, he slid a piece of paper toward me, with the names of some of our clients on it. "Whose clients are these?" he asked.

I replied, "These are my clients."

"How did *you* get these clients?" His tone was more than a little judgmental. I could tell that he really meant, "How could someone who looks like you win these clients?"

I answered, "I just pick up the phone and call people to see if I can help them. Some of them say yes, and I visit them. Some of them give me their orders."

Having grown up working in a small business, I did what I was taught to do—namely, to hustle. When I wasn't interviewing candidates, I called companies that used temporary employees to see if we could help them out.

My new manager thought he had found his new salesperson: me. But I wasn't interested. In fact, I refused to go into sales, believing that selling was something you did *to* someone, not *for* and *with* someone. Certainly, it wasn't something that benefited the party being sold to.

But I found myself up against a wall. My new manager threatened to fire me if I didn't take the role in outside sales. Worried that I wouldn't find another job if he gave me the boot and dreading the idea of being forced to move back to Columbus, I reluctantly took the job as an account executive.

Luckily, my manager was a great mentor and coach. He went on my sales calls with me and took me with him on his. I quickly saw that there was nothing manipulative or self-oriented about anything he did; it was all about finding a way to help the client. Once I discovered that selling was about helping people get a result that they couldn't get without my assistance, I began to love the game. Together, we grew the branch from two thousand hours a week to twenty-two thousand hours a week in billing, making it one of the best and fastest-growing branches of the company in the United States.

I worked in sales and fronted a rock band until 1992, when I had a grand mal seizure while walking up the stairs to my Brentwood apartment. I ended up moving back to Columbus, where I played for a few more years, but the angry, sad grunge rockers led by Nirvana and Pearl Jam had killed the long-haired party rock I loved.

Though my rock career was coming to an end, my at first reluctant sales career was really just starting. As it turns out, I loved selling, too, because it allowed me to be creative and help solve real business problems.

Once I realized my future was in the sales profession, I began to study the discipline seriously. At first, I studied so that I could become more professional and successful as a salesperson. After that, I studied so that I could become a more effective leader of sales forces. Now I study so that I can help other sales leaders improve the performance of their sales forces. As of this writing, I've been studying sales for more than two and a half decades.

Over the years, I've read hundreds of books about sales, and I've explored all of the major concepts, strategies, and tactics in the discipline, often by contacting the very people who pioneered them. I've also had the opportunity to test these ideas in the real world, on my own, and in the larger context of sales organizations.

From the very moment I began, I've been seeking the answer to a single, central question: *Why do a few highly successful salespeople consistently outperform their peers?*

And they do. We've all seen it. We all know salespeople who deliver superlative performances, selling overpriced commodities you wouldn't expect anyone to buy, while others fail at selling the hottest product in the hottest markets. There are, at this very moment, people at incredibly hot companies, like Google or Apple, who aren't making their quotas. And there are countless salespeople selling boring industrial equipment who are crushing their numbers even though you've never heard of their companies or products.

So I ask again: Why do a few highly successful salespeople consistently outperform their peers?

The answer isn't what you might expect. Success in sales isn't situational. In other words, it isn't based on the product you sell, your customer accounts, or your territory. It doesn't depend on the sales process you use or your company's sales executives. It's certainly nice to have a great product, fast-growing accounts, and a virgin territory. It's also important to have an effective sales process and a smart leader on whom you can depend. But there have been successful and unsuccessful salespeople in every situation I've ever seen.

To answer my question correctly, you must understand, again, that sales isn't situational—it's *individual*. Sales success resides in *you*. *You* pick up the phone and call a prospective customer with another new idea, even after being rejected a dozen times before. *You* sit face-to-face with the customer and create value. *You* muster the support needed to ensure that the customer can capture that value.

Nothing carries as much weight in the sales success equation as *you* do.

SOLVING THE SALES EQUATION

So what do you need to succeed—to make sure the sales equation works for you in a powerful way?

Just three things: a mind-set, a skill set, and a tool kit.

I shamelessly stole the idea of mind-set, skill set, and tool kit from my friend Gerhard Gschwandtner, the charismatic publisher of *Selling Power* magazine and, concerning the topics of sales and success, one of the most curious, thoughtful people I know. I don't know where Gerhard came up with this powerful trio, but as soon as I heard it, I knew it was the framework I needed.

Salespeople first need to be equipped with the right mind-set: the right set of beliefs and attitudes. Then they need the right skill set, which is the ability to do all the things good salespeople do—such as prospecting, gaining commitments, and creating value for their prospective clients. Finally, they need the right tool kit, which consists of scripts, playbooks, documented sales processes, and sales methodologies. (Tool kits are highly customized to your business specifically and outside the scope of this book.) Salespeople need those three things, in this order: mind-set, skill set, tool kit. In this book, we'll focus exclusively on mind-set and skill set.

The book you hold in your hand isn't like any other sales book that you might pick up. It isn't based on extensive and expensive research done by a global consulting firm. Nor is it about sales processes or methodologies, even though books that provide those frameworks are extremely useful. It doesn't recount my experiences and adventures in sales (although some short anecdotes do appear between these covers). There is, however, a great deal of discussion about *you* and the mind-set and skill set you need to be successful.

This book is a field guide of sorts: a handbook. I wrote it for salespeople who are deeply interested in improving themselves and their results. I also wrote it to give frontline sales managers a framework for quickly and easily identifying the challenges faced by members of their teams. I believe I will also help sales managers, by giving them a framework they can use to make a difference for the salespeople they have the privilege to serve and to lead.

The first half of the book doesn't even touch on how to sell. Instead, it's all about who you have to be to sell successfully today. Note that the "who" comes before the "how." I don't know of any other sales book that focuses first on mind-set, but I do know that without the right mind-set, all the selling skills in the world won't be nearly as effective as they could be—if they are effective at all.

In the second half of the book, we look at the skills required to sell effectively today—but not *just* the skill sets, for these chapters capture *both* the mind-set and skill set necessary to win deals. In other words, they capture the essential elements of sales success.

After reading—and applying—what you learn in this book, you will be on your way to developing the attributes and attitudes that make you someone worth buying from. You'll also have a deeper understanding of the skills that you need to create value for your clients. With the combined power of the success attributes and the effectiveness gained from developing your sales skills, you will create more sales opportunities. You will also win more of them.

THE ELEMENTS OF SALES SUCCESS

You probably remember the periodic table of elements from your high school chemistry class. The first published version of the table, created in 1869 by a Russian chemist named Dmitri Mendeleev, had 63 named elements. As of this writing, there are 118. We don't know what new elements will be discovered or developed in the future.

Despite my limited knowledge of chemistry, I believe that the periodic table of elements is an excellent metaphor for the concepts in this book, because the elements in the table are the stuff of which our known universe is composed. Everything we are made of and everything we are capable of creating is captured in the table. Just as our entire world is made up of an identifiable set of elements, so too is sales success. My purpose in writing this book is to identify those elements, prioritize them, and assist you in developing them in yourself. I have an ambitious goal: to help you achieve a massive, career-boosting improvement in your sales results. In other words, I want to help you re-create your sales world in the most powerful way possible.

We will do this by utilizing the seventeen elements of the periodic table of sales: elements that create a salesperson's mind-set and skill set. If you master these and use them to remake yourself, you will have everything you need to succeed in sales.

But it's not quite as simple as memorizing a list of items. Remaking yourself doesn't happen overnight. It takes time and effort. You'll see some improvements in your sales results immediately, but mastering the seventeen elements of sales success represents a career's worth of work. Further, like the periodic table of chemical elements, the periodic table of sales is not static. The profession of selling is constantly evolving. The elements of sales success will evolve as our world changes, and new elements will likely be added to the table.

There are two categories of elements in the periodic table of sales, as you might guess: behaviors (mind-set) and skills (skill set). We'll explore the former in part 1 of the book and the latter in part 2.

PART 1—MIND-SET: THE BELIEFS AND BEHAVIORS OF SALES SUCCESS

In part 1, we look at the nine elements that provide you with the ability to create value for others as well as the people skills necessary to achieve outstanding results. These *mind-set* elements are the foundation of your ability to influence prospective clients.

In chapter 1, **Self-Discipline: The Art of "Me Management,"** you will learn to keep the most important commitments: those that you make to yourself. All seventeen elements of sales success—in other words, everything you do—require self-discipline.

In chapter 2, **Optimism: A Positive Mental Attitude**, you will discover how to maintain the optimistic, positive attitude that inspires others to believe that they can improve and find a better future. Optimism also increases your resilience in the face of the inevitable challenges and losses that are part of selling.

Chapter 3, **Caring: The Desire to Help Others**, demonstrates new ways to use genuine caring as a strategic advantage in sales. You'll also learn why there is no conflict between caring and selling effectively.

In chapter 4, **Competitiveness: A Burning Desire to Be the Best**, you'll work on igniting the competitive fire within. You'll develop your strengths, minimize your weaknesses, and learn to compete in a zero-sum game (one in which there can only be one winner).

With chapter 5, **Resourcefulness: Finding a Way or Making One**, we arrive at the linchpin element. In this chapter, you will learn how to spark your imagination and creative genius and discover how to develop the ideas and insights that help you solve your clients' problems. You'll then learn how to apply your newfound resourcefulness to the challenges of prospecting and winning deals.

In chapter 6, **Initiative: Taking Action before It Is Necessary**, you'll discover why being proactive is critical to selling effectively, why it's the heart of prospecting, and why your clients require it of you. We'll crush complacency and replace it with the ability to be proactive, engaged, and innovative.

In chapter 7, **Persistence: Breaking through Resistance**, you'll learn how to a play "the long game." You'll discover how to continue your pursuit of prospective clients without wavering and without becoming a nuisance. You'll become more of a bulldog, but your clients will be grateful that you are.

Chapter 8, **Communication: Listening and Connecting**, is a course in developing your ability to listen and understand and then explain your ideas. The real action in any sale takes place between the buyer and the salesperson, and it all happens through clear communication.

In chapter 9, **Accountability: Owning the Outcomes You Sell**, you'll study the mind-set necessary to execute for your clients. It's no longer enough to drop what you sell at your clients' door. The solution you sold will face its challenges, and your clients will expect you to own them. They're going to hold you accountable for the results you sold. This chapter will give you the action plan you need to deliver for your clients.

Chapter 10, **Mastering the Mind-Set Elements to Create Influence**, summarizes the first nine elements and, crucially, explains why real influence in sales isn't tactical. It's about character. You'll learn how developing each of these first nine elements makes you someone worth buying from, a salesperson who will help your clients take action.

PART 2—SKILL SETS: THE ABILITIES OF SALES SUCCESS

The second part of the book examines the eight skill-set elements of sales success, which enable you to differentiate yourself and your company from your competitors in the hearts and minds of your customers.

Chapter 11 focuses on **Closing: Asking for and Obtaining Commitments**. In order to sell effectively, you have to be able to ask for and obtain commitments. You'll learn how to ask your clients for all the necessary commitments, from the first, the commitment of their time, to the last, the commitment of their business. The need to gain commitments has grown in importance as selling has grown more complex, requiring more commitments from more people.

Prospecting: Opening Relationships and Creating Opportunities follows in chapter 12. If you've been in sales for any length of time, you know that opening is the new closing. In this chapter, you will learn how to improve your ability to prospect effectively as well as boost your desire to do so.

In chapter 13, **Storytelling: Creating and Sharing a Vision**, you'll master the art of writing your clients' stories along with them. You'll learn to make your clients the heroes in their own stories, with you as their guide and partner. And you'll learn to present a better, more compelling story about your future together.

But before you can tell that story, you'll have to know where your prospective client is and wants to go. In chapter 14, **Diagnosing: The Desire to Understand**, you'll learn how to discover the truth of your client's challenges and how to ask the questions that differentiate you, while influencing your client to take action.

Chapter 15, **Negotiating: Creating Win-Win Deals**, explains how to make sure your client receives the benefit of the bargain while ensuring that you capture the value that allows you to deliver.

The three chapters that follow are about skill-set elements of a higher order. You aren't going to find the material we cover in these final chapters covered anywhere like we will cover them here. You won't read much about these elements in the current research on sales either. In the past, these topics weren't always necessary but they're critical today. As our clients' needs have grown more complex and complicated, we have had to develop new skills to create value for them. They're a little tougher to develop than the ones you've been working on already. You'll draw on everything you've learned up to this point to master them.

Chapter 16, **Business Acumen: Understanding Business and Creating Value**, explains why business acumen is the new sales acumen. You'll learn how to develop the ideas, insights, and situational knowledge that underpin your ability to be a relevant and compelling value creator for your clients.

In chapter 17, **Change Management: Building Consensus and Helping Others Change**, you'll learn how to manage all the stakeholder relationships necessary to overcome the status quo. This chapter is a road map to developing and leading change.

Chapter 18 examines **Leadership: Producing Results with and through Others**. You will learn that leadership isn't a title; it's a responsibility. And since you are accountable for producing results, you have to lead both your team *and* your clients.

In the final chapter, **Exercising the Skill-Set Elements to Create a Competitive Advantage**, you'll find the answer to your prospective clients' most challenging question: "Why should I buy from you?" This chapter ties all the elements together and puts them to work in your sales game. You'll find that you've never been more ready or more confident and capable of creating value for your clients and winning deals than you are now.

I know you are anxious to dive in and start developing the elements now. But first we have to define a term I use throughout this book: "dream client."

A dream client is the prospective client for whom you can create breathtaking, jaw-dropping, earth-shattering value and who allows you to keep some of the value that you create (something you know as "profit").

If you want to succeed in sales, you need to focus on prospective clients who have the exact set of challenges you can solve in some unique way that makes you the right partner for them.

I really, really want you to spend your time and energy on dream clients, because your relationship with them produces outsized results. Sometimes in this book, though, I simply use the terms "prospect" or "client." You will still call on prospects and serve some regular clients, but that doesn't mean you shouldn't also focus upstream on your dream clients!

Part 1
MIND-SET: THE BELIEFS AND BEHAVIORS OF SALES SUCCESS

The following ten chapters contain the nine attributes that make up the powerful mind-set you need to succeed in sales today. The tenth and final chapter in this section of the book, "Influence," is the capstone. Influence is what you will have as a result of working on these nine elements.

Let me tell you why this is important and why these elements come before the skill sets.

People still buy from people they know, like, and trust. "Who" you are is more important than "what" you do. The greater risk for you as a salesperson is that you will have the skill sets but not possess the character necessary to create lifetime relationships.

You are more likely to fail in sales from a lack of discipline, a poor attitude, an unwillingness to take initiative, a lack of determination, or a failure to exercise your resourcefulness. We're going to make sure this doesn't happen.

These ten chapters will set you on a lifelong journey. You can continue to grow and develop these attributes for the rest of your life and still have room for improvement. But it won't take you anywhere near that long to start seeing results from improving on each of the nine attributes that make up the sales success mind-set.

Chapter 1

SELF-DISCIPLINE: THE ART OF "ME MANAGEMENT"

Managing yourself is essentially managing your commitments—with others, indeed, but primarily with yourself. And, keeping track of that inventory these days is no simple task. It requires a system—an "external brain"—to keep yourself oriented to be doing the right thing, at the right time.

—David Allen, author of *Getting Things Done*

WHAT'S THE SECRET TO BEING A SUCCESSFUL SALESPERSON? OR a great one?

It's not the product or service you sell. Neither is it your competition, the market environment, your price structure, evolving technology, or any such thing.

It's you. Your ability to manage yourself, to exert self-discipline, spells the difference between success and failure in sales.

Let me rephrase that: self-discipline *is* the difference between success and failure. Yes, there are a lot of other components of the salesperson's mind-set, skill set, and tool kit, but without strong self-discipline, those don't matter one whit.

Most people don't fail because they can't do something. They fail because they aren't *willing* to do what it takes to succeed. This means they aren't willing to discipline themselves. That's why self-discipline, or what I call "me management," is the cornerstone element of sales success. Unless you are willing to take the actions that lead to success, in sales or anything else, it will always elude you.

Self-discipline is the fundamental attribute of all successful people. It allows them to take action even when they don't want to. It makes it possible for them to focus their time and energy on what must be done now, without procrastinating. It gives them the strength to pass up a little pleasure now in exchange for what they really want later. In sales, self-discipline is what separates the great from the mediocre.

It is vital that you take this first element seriously. Don't skip ahead to later chapters, thinking that there is greater value in learning about closing or prospecting. If you work on this one element, if you perfect it, all the others will fall more easily into place.

THE FIRST COMMITMENT

Sales is all about gaining commitments from your prospects. But the most important commitments are those you make to yourself. And you are constantly making commitments to yourself, whether or not you realize it.

For example, you know you need to invest your time prospecting. But the little chime that lets you know an e-mail has arrived has just grabbed your attention again. So instead of making the calls you need to make, you spend an hour looking at your in-box. You've just made a commitment.

The biggest and best prospects in your territory already have someone selling them the same thing you're selling. You know you need to nurture these relationships, and you understand that it will take a well-coordinated, long-term plan to get one of these dream clients to agree to see you—just to *see* you! But you get caught up in office watercooler chatter, and time slips away. You've made another commitment.

It's time to visit a prospective client, but you've been so busy with other things that you didn't review your notes and prepare for the call. Now you are walking into the most important interaction you will ever have with this client without a plan and without some of the things you promised to provide. Yet another commitment.

What are you committing to when you skip your prospecting calls, fail to nurture your relationships, and neglect to prepare?

You are certainly *not* committing to yourself, your future, and your success. And since you did not make and keep these and other commitments, success will be but a dream for you.

WHERE THERE'S A WILL

I discovered the power of self-discipline early in my career. One experience that I've never forgotten occurred on my first day of work after leaving Los Angeles and rejoining the family business in Columbus. That morning, my sales manager walked up to my desk with two minions in tow and dropped a stack of papers in front of me. "These are our accounts, and you are not to call on any of them," she said.

I looked at the stack; there were pages and pages of company names. I was surprised at how many client accounts our little firm had already won. "We are serving all of these companies?" I asked, impressed.

"No!" she snapped. "But *we* are calling on these companies. You are not to call on any of them."

Now I understood: "we" didn't include me.

At 8:00 a.m. the next day, I closed the door to my office and started calling all of the nonexcluded companies listed in the business section of the phone book. I made cold calls until I went to lunch, and when I came back, I made cold calls until the end of the day. I did that the next day and the next and the next. My consistent, disciplined effort was rewarded with face-to-face appointments. The more calls I made, the more appointments I booked. The more appointments I booked, the more business I won. Within six months, I was the sales leader. After twelve months, my sales numbers were higher than those of the rest of the sales team combined. Soon after, the sales manager and her minions left the company.

I am not saying that I was a better salesperson than the other members of the sales team. I am not even saying that I was better at cold calling; I absolutely wasn't. I am saying that disciplined action made the difference between my results and theirs. While I was making calls, my sales manager and her reps were chatting about their weekends, the television shows they had watched the night before, and finding ways to pretend to be busy with existing clients. They were doing anything but prospecting.

My success resulted from nothing more than a willingness to commit to consistent and purposeful action. I forced myself to make thousands of cold calls and, in doing so, I discovered hidden treasures on almost every page of the phone book. It turned out that many of the most lucrative accounts in the city weren't the biggest or best-known companies. They were smaller ones that would never have been included in the list that the sales manager dropped on my desk and told me not to touch.

The sales manager left without understanding what I had done or why I had succeeded. But I learned a lesson that has served me well ever since: self-discipline is essential to sales success. Your good intentions are worthless unless they are coupled with disciplined action.

REAPING THE REWARDS OF ME MANAGEMENT

Effective self-discipline, or me management, depends on three qualities:

1. **Willpower:** You will yourself to act without the prospect of an immediate reward. Countless distractions can divert your attention from what you need to do. It takes willpower to ignore them and stick to

your work, which is sometimes difficult and mundane but always important.

2. **Fortitude:** You display courage in the face of adversity. You often hear "no," but you do not let that discourage you. You find the strength to keep going. You are committed to your chosen course of action, come hell or high water.

3. **Accountability:** You hold yourself accountable for your own results and keep the commitments you make to yourself as if they were commitments made to others. If, for example, you schedule an appointment to meet your dream client, you don't dare miss it or go in unprepared. In fact, unless and until you learn to keep the commitments you make to yourself, you will fail to be accountable for the results you promise to your clients. As Stephen R. Covey, author of *The 7 Habits of Highly Effective People*, put it, "Private victories precede public victories."

FROM THREE COME MORE

Willpower, fortitude, and accountability are the three qualities upon which me management depends. Once you develop these qualities and become a master of self-discipline, you reap many rewards, including the ability to be honest and courageous and to act with integrity. You also discover that greater future rewards are won by delaying gratification. Here's why:

- **Honesty:** It takes willpower to tell the truth, especially when the truth hurts you. We were designed to avoid pain and seek pleasure. Because being honest can sometimes cause you pain, it can require fortitude to act in spite of the personal discomfort, risk, or loss that you may suffer. It's easy to sidestep the difficult conversation or avoid telling the truth, especially when something is your fault and owning up to it may damage your relationships. That's where self-discipline comes in. It allows you to be honest when evasion is the more comfortable choice. And your honesty, your ability to deal with the uncomfortable, makes you more trustworthy and more credible to your clients.

- **Courage:** Courage isn't the absence of fear. It's taking action even though you are gripped by fear. Courage requires the self-discipline to put yourself in harm's way and ignore the internal dialogue that tells you to retreat to safety. Self-discipline gives you the power to be courageous and stand tall, even when you are quaking with fear. It shows that you are committed to something greater, to a higher purpose, and that you are willing to keep that commitment regardless of the price you have to pay.

- **Integrity:** Consistently walking your talk—that is, saying what you mean and meaning what you say—can be tough. But that's the definition of integrity. Your word is your bond, and you can be counted on. It takes willpower, fortitude, and a strong sense of accountability to do what needs to be done, when it needs to be done. Sometimes it's difficult, and sometimes you just don't feel like it. Too often, pleasant distractions threaten to derail you. But self-discipline allows you to keep your word and always walk your talk.

- **Greater future rewards:** The most important benefit of self-discipline is achieving greater rewards down the line by delaying present gratification. You reap nothing now, except maybe some pain, in exchange for a higher return later. For example, instead of luxuriating in the pleasure of nine minutes of extra sleep, you delay that gratification, get up when you should, and arrive at your appointment on time and well prepared, putting yourself head and shoulders above many of your competitors. Or, instead of being dishonest with a client about a mistake you've made and avoiding a little pain right now, you tell the truth, endure the discomfort, and are rewarded later with the client's trust and respect.

In short, willpower, fortitude, and accountability lead to self-discipline. And self-discipline gives you the wherewithal to be honest, act courageously and with integrity, and delay gratification for better returns later. This is why it's so important to master self-discipline, as it's the cornerstone of all the attributes that allow you to succeed.

APPLYING SELF-DISCIPLINE TO ROUTINE MAINTENANCE

We humans are novelty-seeking creatures, attracted to anything that is new, interesting, or exciting. In sales, it's true that some new tools and ideas can revolutionize your efforts and produce exciting results. These are certainly worth looking into. However, much of your success depends on simple, routine maintenance—that is, keeping your nose to the grindstone.

Many salespeople shy away from routine maintenance because it's not terribly exciting or new, and it guarantees that they'll hear "no" over and over again. But routine maintenance does produce predictable results, especially over the long run. It is the first area in which self-discipline must be applied.

THE ROUTINE MAINTENANCE OF PROSPECTING

Here's a basic law of the sales universe: the more desperate you are to fill your pipeline with opportunities, the more difficult it is to do so. You must be vigilant about prospecting on a daily basis so that you don't become desperate. Sporadic prospecting leads to stress, missed commitments, and anxiety that forces you to take on something less than your dream client. But when you are self-disciplined, with the willpower and fortitude to keep prospecting day after day, week after week, month after month, you are practically guaranteed a pipeline full of opportunities.

Make the commitment to attend to the routine maintenance of prospecting every day. In sales, you must continually open new relationships. Remember, no opportunity is ever closed that hasn't first been opened.

THE ROUTINE MAINTENANCE OF NURTURING

To succeed in sales, you must develop the necessary relationships *before* you need them.

Nurturing your dream clients is perhaps the most important activity you can undertake in pursuit of success—but nurturing and urgency don't mix. Once you find yourself desperate for opportunities, it's already too late to develop them. There is no way to rush relationships, and there is no way to rush trust. Both trust and relationships require time and careful, determined, and active attention.

Nurturing relationships, like prospecting, shouldn't be done sporadically if you want to produce predictable, profitable results. Nurturing as a part of routine maintenance builds trust and solidifies the relationships you need, before you need them.

THE ROUTINE MAINTENANCE OF EXISTING CLIENT RELATIONSHIPS

You made promises to your existing clients back when they were just your dream clients, and you have since kept those promises. But that's not enough. Resting on your laurels is a recipe for disaster.

When your clients' needs change, or when the world throws something unexpected at them, you need to be there either to help them overcome the obstacles or capitalize on these new opportunities. Not being there and not proactively working to anticipate and adapt to their changing needs invites client dissatisfaction—the same kind of dissatisfaction that created an opportunity for you to work with your dream client in the first place.

Routine maintenance of your existing relationships demonstrates to your clients that you are a proactive partner for the long term and that you care enough always to walk your talk.

Prospecting, nurturing, and remaining proactive with existing clients are just a few of the areas that require a disciplined routine of maintenance. You could add other items, such as following up, updating your sales-force automation or customer-relationship manager, and sending thank-you cards. Take care of routine daily maintenance, and routine daily maintenance will take good care of you.

FIVE WAYS TO DEVELOP SELF-DISCIPLINE

Wait. You didn't think this was the kind of book you just passively read, did you? No, no, no. At the end of each chapter, you are going to dig in and start applying what you've learned!

Let's look at five ways you can immediately improve your me-management skills and strengthen your willpower, fortitude, and accountability:

1. Create a Discipline List.

You may have written out your goals on occasion, but it is unlikely that you have written a discipline list.

A discipline list is a list of things you do forever because attending to them is continually necessary to produce the results you desire. It differs from a goals list: goals are things you want to achieve, outcomes you strive toward during a certain time period. Goals are either achieved or not achieved by a certain date. But a discipline *has no end*. A discipline list breaks your goals down into actionable steps, concrete things you can do to attain your goals.

A discipline list goes far beyond goals. Running a marathon is a goal; exercising every day is a discipline. Lacking the discipline of daily exercise, a lot of people abandon the routines that built their capacity to run long distances once the marathon is complete. Losing weight is a goal; it isn't the same as the discipline of regularly eating healthy, low-calorie meals to fuel your ongoing performance. The same idea applies to sales.

Your discipline list might include spending the first hour of each day making calls to the hottest leads on your list, the best prospects in your territory, and the referrals you've picked up from existing clients. Other disciplines might be preparing for your sales calls before every client interaction and following up every client visit with a thank-you note.

Start developing your me-management skills by creating a discipline list that breaks your goals down into actionable steps. Then decide whether the steps need to be completed on a daily, weekly, or monthly basis, and schedule them accordingly. Don't make your discipline list too long; you don't have to do everything every day.

Let's say one of your goals is to identify more new sales opportunities. You might choose a couple of disciplines that ensure that you achieve this goal. Your discipline for that goal might be to prospect one hour a day, every day, every week, every year, for as long as you're in sales. In the long run, one week of active prospecting can't possibly bring about the positive results achieved through one hour of prospecting per day, forever. You might try a second discipline: sending one piece of content that your prospective client would find valuable to each prospect every month for twelve months with a handwritten note. Making calls for an hour a day and sending a personal note each month are not goals; they're disciplines.

When you have completed your discipline list, look at the various items and add up the results they should produce. Are the results great enough to achieve your goals? If not, rework the list until they are.

You can download a free discipline work sheet at www.theonlysales guide.com.

2. Do the Worst Things First.

You often face unpleasant or difficult tasks. And you're always tempted to put them off by doing just about anything else that needs to be done—and sometimes things that don't need to be done! Unfortunately, avoiding the tough stuff is a recipe for failure.

Instead of delaying your most difficult tasks, attend to them first thing in the morning, while you are still fresh and before the world starts distracting you with its demands. Finishing a difficult task gives you a burst of energy and makes it easier to tackle the next task. This is also a surefire way to build success momentum.

Your discipline list will undoubtedly contain tasks that you dislike or find difficult. Identify them and then schedule them as early in your day as possible. Right now, you can probably think of some dreaded task that is critical to a desired result. Open your calendar and put it on tomorrow morning's schedule. Then be sure to complete it before you do anything else that day.

One of the disciplines that I dread is exercising. I have to get up, get dressed, drive to the gym, and lift heavy weights. If I don't work out first thing in the morning, it's easy to make excuses and forgo my commitment to my health. So I wake up at 5:00 a.m. and work out at 5:30 a.m. every day. Once I am at the gym, I am reminded that the greatest resistance isn't the weights that I lift. It's the internal resistance of getting to the gym in the first place.

Have you ever had to make a call to a client or prospect that you knew was going to be difficult? If you haven't, I promise you will. The longer you wait to make important calls to resolve a major issue, the worse the issue becomes. Waiting to make the call also increases the likelihood that your tough call becomes even more challenging.

Make that call first. Do it, and get it over with first thing in the morning. No matter the outcome (which, in my experience, is almost always better than I hoped for), you will be more productive the rest of the day.

3. Make Your Commitments in Writing.

Putting all your commitments in writing can have a powerful effect on your ability to keep the promises you make to yourself. Writing out your disciplines moves them from the ephemeral to the concrete; it takes them out of the world of ideas and makes them real.

Put your commitments down in writing. To make the exercise even more powerful, include the following lists:

- **Positive outcomes you'll enjoy when you fulfill your commitments.** List ways in which your sales results, career, and quality of life will improve. These will remind you of the rewards that await you and will motivate you to keep your promises.
- **Negative things that will happen if you fail to honor your commitments.** List the ways in which failure will affect your results and how these results will impact your professional development and other areas of your life. This list will remind you of the risks you take when you fail to keep your promises, and it will motivate you to avoid that pain.

For example, if you make the commitment to prospect for the first hour every day, the positive outcomes you will enjoy will include making more connections, creating new opportunities, building a bigger and better pipeline of opportunities, and, eventually, winning more opportunities. Maybe the biggest positive outcome here is greater income and the ability to provide a better life for yourself and your family.

What happens if you fail to keep this commitment and don't make your calls? You'll know fewer people, have fewer real connections, create too few opportunities, and fail to generate the new business you need. The biggest pain you may suffer is a lack of income—or, carried to the most extreme conclusion, maybe the loss of your job. That's pain!

Your long-term motivation is found in the reasons you are taking these actions. These written commitments, with their positive and negative consequences, provide you with a bigger "why."

4. Make Your Commitments Public.

If you're like most people, you care about what others think of you. So, if you publicly declare that you will do something, you'll try harder to follow through. You'll also pay a steep price for failing to fulfill these public promises, as you will destroy others' confidence and trust in you. Making your commitments public can do much to motivate you to become more self-disciplined.

If you plan to prospect daily, which I highly recommend, publish your prospecting calendar as a way to gain support from your peers. Post the calendar on your door. Or, if you have shared calendars, schedule an appointment with yourself so that your peers can see the time you have blocked. Then take it further and share your discipline list with your peers and your manager. You can ratchet up your self-discipline and the pressure to perform by making these commitments public.

It takes courage to make public commitments, but if you do, you'll reap even greater rewards by earning the confidence and trust of others when you keep these promises.

5. Eliminate Distractions and Stop Multitasking.

Self-discipline is not easily achieved, and life is so rife with distractions that it can seem as if the world were conspiring against you. You probably find yourself doing several things at once—like making calls while browsing the Internet, or clicking through e-mails in real time while you are supposed to be following up on your prior week's meeting—and not really focusing on any one thing for any length of time. Some people claim that multitasking helps them accomplish more, but according to the latest neuroscience research, multitasking splinters your attention and decreases brainpower. You end up doing less effective work while needing more time to complete it.

As you work through your discipline list, eliminate all distractions and concentrate on one task at a time. Turn off your cell phone, close the Web browser, hang a **DO NOT DISTURB** sign on your doorknob, and devote all your attention and brainpower to achieving your goals.

THE FIRST ELEMENT: THE POWER STEP

Make me management the cornerstone of your personal success formula. Work hard to increase your self-discipline—your willpower, fortitude, and accountability—the foundation of all behaviors and skills that makes you a master salesperson. Start today by making commitments to yourself—and keeping them.

FIRST MOVE—DO THIS NOW!

What is the one thing that you need to do now that you have put off or resisted doing? Is it a phone call you need to make to your dream client to schedule an appointment? Is it a follow-up call you need to make to a client who you know is unhappy with you or your company? Whatever it is, do it now.

By taking the actions you need to take when you need to take them, you build the discipline necessary to succeed in sales.

RECOMMENDED READING

Allen, David. *Getting Things Done: The Art of Stress-Free Productivity*. New York: Penguin Group USA, 2015.

Covey, Stephen R., Roger A. Merrill, and Rebecca R. Merrill. *First Things First*. West Valley City, UT: Franklin Covey, 2015.

Leonard, George. *Mastery: The Keys to Success and Long-Term Fulfillment*. New York: Penguin Group USA, 1992.

Chapter 2

OPTIMISM: A POSITIVE MENTAL ATTITUDE

It's good to follow your passion. It's better to bring it with you.

—Jeb Blount, author of *People Buy You*

SELLING IS AN ACTION-ORIENTED ENDEAVOR. YOU MAKE CALLS, set schedules, prepare presentations, and write up proposals; you meet, strategize, negotiate, and more. It feels like sales is all about action, movement, and momentum—and it is.

But most of that action is completely worthless without a positive mental attitude, without optimism.

Action produces results for you and your clients—problems solved, profits made. But without the right mental attitude, your actions will be feeble and fleeting. Optimism allows you to perform powerfully and consistently in a coordinated manner over the long run. Optimism ensures that you'll stay focused on your task, despite the lows that inevitably follow some of the highs.

OPTIMISM VERSUS PESSIMISM

To succeed in sales, you must have, or develop, optimism. A pessimistic attitude in sales will be your undoing. Pessimism kills success because it kills initiative. If you're pessimistic, it will seem like sheer lunacy to pick up the phone and call a prospective customer who has refused to see you for years. After all, this prospective customer has never even let you out of the starting gate. You'll assume that, once again, you'll be rejected. If you're pessimistic, you'll be convinced that your competitors have long-term contracts and meaningful relationships with their customers and that you can't sway them with whatever value you're offering. "If the customers will keep buying from my competitors," you'll tell yourself, "and nothing can change that, why bother trying?" And success will elude you.

Pessimism undermines your self-discipline and the purposeful action you must take to succeed. It disempowers you by providing you with the excuses to give up. The pessimistic mind-set always finds a way to rationalize decisions, like not making your calls, and absolves you of responsibility, thus protecting your ego. Consider the following pessimistic statements. Have you ever said any of these to yourself or, heaven forbid, to someone else?

- "The economy isn't good, and no one is buying right now." (This is a statement you know to be false because countless salespeople are crushing it right now.)
- "My territory is crummy and all the best prospects are taken." (Yet you also know that "it's not the land, it's the man," and that salespeople with the right attitude can produce results within your territory.)
- "My sales manager prevents me from succeeding." (You know that your sales manager isn't standing next to you, preventing you from picking up your phone and dialing.)
- "My commission structure is my real problem." (Your real problem is that you aren't doing the work necessary for your commission structure to become an issue.)

- "My competitors always beat me on price." (This is a lie we tell ourselves when we fail to create enough value to differentiate ourselves and produce a win.)

If you're telling yourself any of these things, you're allowing pessimism to destroy your ability and willingness to take action. Even if some of these things are true—even if your territory isn't very good and your commission structure is problematic—when you tell yourself these things, you're allowing pessimism to guide your thoughts and your actions. Or lack of action, as the case may be.

Optimism, on the other hand, thrusts you forward. Optimism is the belief that things will work out for the best, that you can win against all odds. It is the conviction that you can make a positive difference in the world and that, because of it, you will be rewarded. Optimism keeps you going by helping you remember that the next call you make may be the one that finally convinces your dream client to meet with you. It is the conviction that eventually something will change, and you'll get that long-sought-after opportunity to win the customer's business. Optimism enables you to confront and overcome all obstacles and challenges. It gives you the power to persist.

OPTIMISM AND THE BELIEFS OF SALES SUCCESS

A lot of people think that optimism is inborn: you either have it or you don't. While it may be true that some people enter this world with a tendency toward either optimism or pessimism, I believe that you can train yourself to become as optimistic as you need to be. You can be full of enthusiasm and hope for the future, certain that good things are bound to happen, and convinced that you *will* achieve your desired outcome, even when there is little or no evidence to support this conviction.

We humans have met almost every challenge thrown our way. We have eradicated diseases that once killed millions. We have bridged vast distances, even sending people to the moon and hurling space probes billions of miles to the very boundaries of our solar system. History books are filled with stories of people overcoming seemingly insurmountable obstacles, achieving mostly because they believed they could, even in the face of impossible odds.

Most of our day-to-day challenges, naturally, are not quite so heroic (although I have won a couple of deals that felt more difficult than orchestrating a Mars landing). But that just means that our obstacles are more easily overcome. To meet any challenge, however, you must first believe that you can. Every challenge successfully met begins with a vision, and that vision is driven by optimism.

You *must* be optimistic enough to envision success. Optimism is a springboard to a better future. It also underlies the four beliefs that you must hold in order to sell successfully:

Belief #1: I make a difference.

Your success depends on your belief that your efforts will produce value for your customers, your company, and yourself. This faith is a tremendous source of power and initiative. When you believe that you can make a difference and you are a value creator, your confidence and feelings of self-worth will soar. You will be empowered to take action.

Belief #2: I will succeed.

The more you believe in your success, the more motivated you are to achieve it. To put it another way, you get what you expect. If you expect success, you will find a way to achieve it. If you expect failure, you can't help but act in a way that ensures it. Guess which outcome the optimist expects?

This belief, "I will succeed," not only drives positive outcomes but also forms the foundation of your willingness to persevere—an absolutely essential trait for any salesperson.

Belief #3: People will help me.

Believing that other people will support you in the pursuit of your goals is a powerful enabler. It reminds you that you are not alone in this world. It gives you the confidence to ask for help and to accept it when it is offered. Belief in the helpfulness of others also enhances your ability to be resourceful in your quest.

Being resourceful, as I explain in chapter 5, is critical. You will find people who are eager to help you once you believe that they exist and you start asking for help.

Belief #4: Things will go wrong yet still work out in the end.

Winston Churchill said, "Success is the ability to go from one failure to another with no loss of enthusiasm." The ability to bounce back after a string of failures is based on the belief that you may not always get the outcome you expect, but if you continue working toward your goals, eventually you will get the results you seek. This is the source of perseverance.

When you are optimistic, you gladly take ownership of your failures and use them to improve your outcomes. As an optimist, you respond to failure in three ways:

1. **Accept it.** You don't blame the economy, your sales manager, your territory, or your competitors. Instead, you accept that you, and you alone, are responsible for your results.
2. **Embrace it.** You embrace the fact that your actions landed you where you are right now. Once you embrace responsibility for your results, you create the power to change them. If your past actions are to blame, then your future actions can produce different results. Embracing responsibility empowers you.
3. **Learn from it.** Failure offers you powerful lessons and provides you with the information you need to make changes. Analyze the

situation carefully. What you did in the past is, obviously, what *not* to do. What does that tell you about what you *should* do? The answers are right in front of you.

Optimists don't believe that the act of failing makes them failures. Failure is simply an event. It doesn't define you or your future. Failure provides feedback on a performance and creates an opportunity to improve.

FIVE WAYS TO DEVELOP OPTIMISM

Now let's work on building your optimistic, positive, empowered mind-set:

1. Keep a Gratitude Journal.

If you are naturally pessimistic, you just groaned when you read "gratitude journal." But if you're an optimist, you thought, "I knew it!"

Being grateful is one of the most empowering choices you can make. That's because gratitude and optimism go hand in hand, and it's literally impossible to be grateful and pessimistic at the same time. Start by listing all of the good things in your life—the things that make you happy.

I recommend starting your practice by writing down three things for which you are grateful.

Look, it's easy to start with the people you love and the people that love you. You can write that down and remind yourself as often as you like. That said, you have a lot of things to be grateful for that you likely take for granted, like your health, the person who mentored you in college, the mistake you made that taught you a life lesson that transformed the direction of your life, that you live in a time of incredible opportunity, or something as simple as the technology that enables us to live the way we live now.

As you practice gratitude, your ability to be grateful for smaller things will grow.

Once you've created your initial list, take a minute or two each morning to add to it. Hang the list on your bathroom mirror to remind you of what you have to be thankful for.

Visit www.theonlysalesguide.com *to download a free gratitude journal and a list of prompts to get you started.*

2. Keep a Record of the Value You Create.

Remind yourself of your ability to make a difference in the world by keeping a record of the value you have created for others. Everyone has a record of success; use yours to bolster your optimism. It will come in handy as you prepare not only for sales calls but also for performance reviews, salary negotiations, and job interviews. Here are the key steps to tracking the value you create:

- List all of your accomplishments, including the specific results you've delivered to your customers and your company, in both qualitative and quantitative terms. No accomplishment is too small.
- Include the value you have brought to your sales engagements. How did your training and development help you help your clients? How did your knowledge and experience benefit a client with a particularly difficult challenge? How has your insight helped your clients?

You have succeeded in the past, and you will succeed in the future. Like the time you helped a client solve a problem they believed was unsolvable. Or the time you gained an appointment with the unreachable C-level executive who never takes calls from salespeople, opening the opportunity that eventually won you your dream client. Reminding yourself of who you are and the value you create bolsters your optimistic attitude.

3. Discard Unhealthy Beliefs.

Before you can develop a more optimistic mind-set, you may have to shed some old beliefs.

Most people have at least a few unhealthy beliefs. Maybe you believe that your efforts can't make a difference, that your past losses are indicative of your future performance, or that external forces will inevitably sabotage your success. Sometimes these beliefs are so entrenched that they operate at an unconscious level; you may not even know they exist.

The first step to rooting out unhealthy beliefs is to articulate them. Pick one area where you aren't taking sufficient action right now. Write down the belief that is preventing you from acting and describe the results it produces. Then discard each belief that produces negative results by creating a new, more optimistic and empowering belief to replace it. Write it down.

Here's an unhealthy belief worth tackling in a book on sales success. A lot of people believe that cold calling no longer works and that their efforts won't produce new opportunities. Because they read advertisements and pitches from companies who sell technology designed to replace the need to make calls that center on the idea that "cold calling is dead," they harbor unhealthy beliefs about making calls.

That belief is unhealthy, and it will prevent you from creating the opportunities you need. As you'll discover later, a healthier belief is that "all prospecting methods have value, and that having more options to reach prospects is better than having fewer." This belief reflects the truth, provides you with more options, and leads to greater success.

This new belief should spur you to take new action. Write down what that action might be, and then do it!

Being aware that you need to take action and yet refusing to take it brings the same results as being unaware. Use your knowledge to change your behavior.

If you find that you have trouble identifying and discarding unhealthy beliefs, ask people you trust, such as your family, friends, colleagues, or mentors, to share their observations about your beliefs and the resulting actions you take (or fail to take).

4. Avoid Cynics, Critics, Slackers, and Burnouts.

When you were young, your parents were probably concerned about whom you hung around with. They wanted you to have the "right" friends. When I was a teenager playing rock and roll in bars at night, I had the kind of friends who gave my mother plenty to worry about!

There's a good reason that your parents worried about the people you spent time with. Your peers reinforce a certain psychology, a certain set of beliefs, and certain kinds of behaviors. What concerned your parents should now concern you because the people you spend time with can build you up or pull you down.

Think about the people you spend the most time with both at work and outside of work. Then ask yourself whether they reinforce the positive or the negative in you.

- **Positive reinforcers:** Some people support your belief that you are capable of more, that you can be more. They reinforce your positive personal psychology, empowering you and supporting you. These people are positive reinforcers. They inspire you, and they challenge you to expand your horizons and do better.
- **Negative reinforcers:** These people intensify your fears and may supply you with new ones. They have a scarcity mind-set, believing that there is never enough because someone else has more. Negative reinforcers are naysayers and cynics who steal your dreams, lower the bar, and never see the silver lining. They hold you back.

Spend as much time as possible with positive reinforcers, and avoid negative reinforcers like the plague. You are responsible for your personal psychology, for your mind-set, and you must protect it. You may not recognize these negative influences working to destroy your personal psychology because they often work at the subconscious level. But, I assure you, they are all around you.

Negativity is the only cancer that spreads by contact. The more you are exposed to negative people, the greater the risk of infection. To maintain your positive attitude, identify and avoid cynics, critics, slackers, and burnouts. They're easy to spot:

- Cynics do not believe in anything. They do not believe that their company is special or that it creates value.
- Critics believe that everybody in the company and all of the customers are wrong. Instead of working to make things better, they throw grenades at the people who try. They can kill your motivation.
- Slackers believe they are overworked and underpaid. They keep a low profile, do as little work as possible, and try to skate by unnoticed. They sap your time and resources.
- Burnouts are tired. Whatever passion they once possessed has long since been extinguished. They are just killing time and don't want you to work too hard because it makes them look bad.

If you sleep with dogs, you wake up with fleas. Negative people can easily infect your mind-set and destroy your positivity. Stay away from them as much as possible.

5. Go on a Negativity Fast.

We all know that "garbage in" results in "garbage out." Despite this, we are barraged with fear, negativity, and scarcity. News programs carry a steady stream of negativity, and much of what you find on the Internet is sensationalism and gossip. Our lives are filled with opportunities to wallow in the negative, and it can be hard to resist the temptation to do so.

You can improve your attitude and become more optimistic by going on a negativity fast. For the next thirty days, do not watch, listen to, or read the news. Avoid negative and sensationalized media. Ignore all gossip about misbehaving reality stars and their ilk; there is nothing positive there. Avoid all negative people whenever possible. Refuse to say anything negative or engage in conversations with a negative slant. Think only positive thoughts. If a negative thought enters your mind, replace it with a positive one immediately.

As part of your negativity fast, you'll need a plan for dealing with people in your life, many of whom love and care about you. You should have your response ready when a coworker corners you to complain for the hundredth time about the new compensation plan. For example, you might say, "Listen, I am happy to discuss this with you, but let's not get into complaining. Our focus should be on the actions we should take to remedy the situation." You'll be surprised how your attitude improves, and how optimistic you can become by avoiding as much negativity as possible.

FROM THOUGHTS TO ACTION

Sales is all about action, and actions result from thoughts. Optimistic thoughts lead to optimistic action, while pessimistic thoughts lead to self-defeating action or none at all. You are not a victim of whatever pops into your head. You can choose your own thoughts and replace those that don't serve your purpose. Choose to think optimistic thoughts about yourself, your career, and your ability to succeed. Optimism—a combination of hope, belief, and confidence—empowers you. Your optimistic mind-set will ensure that, inevitably, you will prevail.

FIRST MOVE—DO THIS NOW!

This isn't an easy assignment, but it's necessary. You are going to have to become aware of your inner critic, that negative voice that is always speaking to you in negative terms (and whose negativity you often repeat). Your inner critic sometimes says things like, "This sucks" or "I

---

hate this." It also reminds you, "You're not good at this" or "You can't do that. You'll embarrass yourself."

When you hear these thoughts, write them down, and then write the response from your inner coach. Your inner coach might say, "You've got this" or "It's all you." Instead of telling yourself that something "sucks" or that you hate it, try, "It's nowhere near as bad as people make it out to be" or "This is the work that separates the professionals from the pretenders." Start choosing empowering thoughts and words. You'll find that they lead to empowering beliefs.

RECOMMENDED READING

Achor, Shawn. *The Happiness Advantage: The Seven Principles of Positive Psychology That Fuel Success and Performance at Work*. New York: Crown Business, 2010.

Frankl, Viktor. *Man's Search for Meaning*. Boston: Beacon Press, 2006.

Ridley, Matt. *The Rational Optimist: How Prosperity Evolves*. New York: HarperCollins, 2010.

Chapter 3

CARING: THE DESIRE TO HELP OTHERS

All things being equal, people will do business with, and refer business to, those people they know, like, and trust.

—Bob Burg, author of *The Go-Giver*

SELLING HAS BECOME MORE DIFFICULT OVER THE PAST COUPLE of decades. Your clients and dream clients are under more pressure to produce greater results with fewer resources, and the demand for financial performance takes precedence above all else. As a result, your clients and dream clients expect more from you. They need you to have the business acumen to help them make positive change and produce better results. The skills necessary to handle tough selling situations will become even more important in the future.

Yet some things never change. Certain universal truths remain, regardless of changes in the economy, technology, and society. One is that clients still buy from those they know, like, and trust. And they tend to like and trust those who care about them. *Genuinely* care about them.

Let's say that two salespeople are selling to the same organization. The first one has the better solution—but the prospective client doesn't know this salesperson well because he hasn't visited often, even though he has sent numerous e-mails and other materials. During one of his infrequent visits, the salesperson made a few references to the commission he stood to make. These mentions were brief—fleeting, really—but they were there. And since the prospect doesn't know the salesman, she doesn't know whether or not she can trust him.

Meanwhile, the second salesperson's solution isn't quite as good, but this fellow has spent a fair amount of time inside the prospect's company, asking questions and occasionally offering ideas. The prospect knows him, and she and her team trust him. He's been willing to talk about the challenges they will need to face together to produce better results. He's also personable; the client likes him and would gladly have him as part of her team.

It shouldn't surprise you when the client decides to go with the second salesperson.

All things being equal, relationships win. Even when all things are unequal, relationships still win. That's why your job in sales depends on building relationships that, in turn, are built on caring, empathizing with your clients, and helping them. *Truly* helping them.

Has a prospective client ever asked you to present your solution one more time after your competitor made a case that should have clinched the deal? Has your dream client ever revealed your competitor's price and solution so you could revise your own? When this happens—and it happens a lot—it is because you are known, liked, and trusted. Your clients feel that you care about them.

CARING IS THE KEY TO RELATIONSHIPS

A successful sales career is built around customers who believe that you care about them—who recognize that your top priority is not *your* gain, but *theirs*. They know that not only will you create positive outcomes for them, you will be there for them until they achieve those outcomes.

CARING: THE DESIRE TO HELP OTHERS

My friend Charlie Green, coauthor of *The Trusted Advisor* and the foremost authority on the value of trust in selling, developed an equation that illustrates the value of good relationships:

Trust = (Credibility x Reliability x Intimacy) / Self-Orientation

The second half of the right side of the equation reads "divided by Self-Orientation." This means that the more you focus on yourself and your bottom line, the more you lower your credibility, reliability, and intimacy with prospective clients—in other words, the less you are trusted.

It doesn't matter how believable you are when expounding on your product, service, or solution. It doesn't matter if J. D. Power and Associates says you work for the most reliable firm in your industry. If your primary interest is yourself, you will be liked and trusted less and have weaker relationships with your clients and prospective clients.

As the opposite of self-orientation, caring is the sincere desire to understand others, to create positive outcomes for them, and to devote energy to achieving those outcomes. It is the deep desire that your customers receive all the value and benefits that you sell to them. When you care about others, you'll work hard to understand them, look out for their interests, and invest yourself in their success. When you truly care, you will move mountains to help others.

But you cannot simply tell people that you care; you must show them. You prove it by repeatedly taking actions that benefit your customer: by bringing together the resources needed to produce value for your customer, by presenting solutions worth buying *before* you ask for a sale, and by delivering valuable ideas. Most of all, you prove that you care through the actions you take *after* the sale—when you orchestrate and ensure the delivery of value, take the call if something goes wrong, and immediately work to resolve any problems.

You can't fake caring—or at least not for long. You have probably had salespeople fool you into believing they had your best interests at heart.

But it usually doesn't take long to realize their true motivations. Once you do, if you are like me, you probably choose to do business with someone else.

THE THREE ELEMENTS OF CARING

Caring is the desire to understand others and create positive outcomes for them. In order to do this, you must be as follows:

- **Empathetic:** Being empathetic means putting yourself in another's position and feeling what she feels. An empathetic salesperson takes the time to explore clients' thoughts and emotions, to gain a deeper understanding of their situations and mind-sets. This creates the foundation of a caring customer connection.
- **Intimate:** Unless you sell the least expensive offering on the market, you'll need to deliver added value. The only way to add value is to cultivate a deep understanding of your customers' needs and develop solutions that fit those needs exactly. This requires intimacy, a close, personal bond formed through knowledge and experience of another.
- **Present:** Caring requires that you be present. When you make face-to-face sales calls, your presence at the client's place of business is proof that you care. When you take the time to meet with your clients to ensure that what you sold them is working, or simply to learn more about their business, you prove that you care. Even if your work is done via phone or Web conference, you need to demonstrate that you are present. Find ways to engage your clients in conversation while on the phone or online to demonstrate that you are present and mindful.

Just as presence is a powerful way to demonstrate that you care, absence is an equally powerful demonstration of the opposite. Absence does *not* make the heart grow fonder—it makes it wander. It sends a clear message that the client is not important enough to command your time. More clients are lost to neglect than to any other cause.

All three components of caring came into play in my relationship with a client who was tough, mean, and had an amazing ability to pepper every utterance with curse words. No one wanted to work with her, but I had just moved into a new territory and needed her business. No matter how unpleasant she was, I kept going back. She cursed at me when things went wrong and "only" yelled at me when things went well. But through it all, I kept showing up. I was present.

One day as I was sitting in her office, her expression suddenly shifted from angry to sad, and she said, "I don't know how much more of this I can take. I work fourteen hours here each day, and then I spend the night in the hospital with my husband. He has cancer and has already had two operations."

I couldn't relate to her experience. But she needed someone to listen, and I was willing to imagine myself in her position and try to feel what she felt. I'm not sure anyone had truly listened to her before. By being empathetic, I was able to establish a sort of intimacy with her.

After that, our relationship changed. She was still tough, mean, and cursed at everyone she worked with. She likely still frightened off every one of my competitors. But she was nicer to me.

Empathy, intimacy, and presence—when you develop and demonstrate these three traits, your customers will know that you care.

FOCUS ON CARING; THE OUTCOME WILL FOLLOW

A decade ago, Tim Sanders, then Yahoo's chief solutions officer and leadership coach, wrote a book called *Love Is the Killer App* in which he argued that we need to become "lovecats." Being a lovecat means sharing knowledge, networks, and compassion in order to make ourselves indispensable. It's a great idea: treating sales as an act of caring. I know this kind of "squishy" talk can make tough road warriors uncomfortable, but caring is a trait that all salespeople, tough or not, must develop.

Your intentions matter, and they are felt by your clients, your prospects, and all of the people with whom you interact. When you come from a place of caring, you generate trust and build powerful relationships. But if your actions are self-serving, they destroy trust and ruin relationships.

Caring doesn't just help your clients; it also empowers you as a salesperson. When you care about producing better results for your prospects, you *know* you're doing the right thing by selling those results. There's no self-doubt, no second-guessing yourself, no hesitation to make the call: you know you're helping. When you care enough about your customers to ensure that they get their desired outcomes, you never have to blame yourself for losing their business.

When you know you are doing the right thing, the outcome of the sale matters less. It sounds paradoxical, but it's true: your sales effectiveness is inversely proportional to the intensity of your focus on your own results. The more egocentric you are—that is, the more focused you are on earning your commissions, boosting your sales results, and making your numbers—the less likely you are to achieve your goals. Conversely, the more outwardly focused and customer-centric you are, the faster you increase your commissions, improve your sales results, and make your numbers.

Make no mistake about it: Your clients can sense your intentions. They can tell if you are self-oriented, seeking only personal gain. They can also tell if you are truly customer focused, working to help them produce the results they need. I'm sure you've sat across from a salesperson who wasn't really listening to you, and you instantly knew her only intention was to sell you. Or, conversely, you've met a salesperson so focused on your needs that you knew immediately you were going to work with him. In both cases, you could feel the salesperson's intentions.

If this talk of intentions is too soft for you, ask yourself which salesperson you would want to call on your aging parents or grandparents: one who really cares about her customers or one who is focused on herself? Which salesperson are you going to be?

It's a simple truth: the more you care about your customer's results, the better your own results will be. And caring is infectious. When you care about your customers, your customers care about you. If you run into trouble executing your solutions or delivering outcomes, your customers won't bail on you. Instead, they will help you solve the problem.

This is why I call caring the "killer sales app." It doesn't matter that your company is smaller than your competitors' or that your competitors' solutions have shiny bells and whistles that yours lack. Caring always levels the playing field.

Bottom line: your dream clients will choose the salesperson they believe cares the most about them and about helping them to achieve success. That's why you need to care about your prospects and customers *more* than your competitors do.

FIVE WAYS TO TURN CARING INTO A COMPETITIVE ADVANTAGE

OK, I know you're tough as nails. But it's time to lighten up a bit and open yourself up to being a little softer, unlocking the better version of yourself that is here to make a difference for others. Here are some ways to increase your ability to care for others:

1. Be a Student of People.

To empathize with your customers, you must understand what they are feeling. To get insight into how they feel, pay careful attention to their verbal cues and body language. Is your dream client sitting with a scowl on her face and her arms crossed when you talk to her? Or is her face softened, showing that she's open to your ideas? Listen to the words the client uses, especially the emotionally charged words. For example, does he say he's "pissed off" or "miffed"? Does she use a charged word like "furious" or the more neutral "disappointed"? What do these words indicate the client is feeling?

Deciphering these cues takes practice, but it's an understanding that's worth your time. If you want to learn more about reading people's body language, pick up *What Every Body Is Saying: An Ex-FBI Agent's Guide to Speed-Reading People* by Joe Navarro.

When you know what your customer is feeling, you will be better able to respond appropriately, to connect, and to communicate in a way that demonstrates your caring.

2. Imagine Yourself in the Customer's Position.

Don't just think about what your customer is feeling. Put yourself in his position and *feel* what he is feeling. Would you be angry? Would you be excited about a new opportunity? What would you need? What would you do?

It takes real compassion to occupy the position of another person, and the ability to do so can take years to develop—it's not as easy as it sounds. Empathy demands practice, but the results are worth it.

Empathy creates connections and lays a foundation of trust; it puts you on your customer's side.

3. Listen to and Accept the Customer's Interpretation.

Caring requires that you not only listen to others but also accept that their interpretations of events, facts, or ideas are true *for them*. Listen without passing judgment on either the facts or the meaning of what the customer says, and accept her interpretation as valid and worthwhile.

In sales, we spend a lot of time trying to change people's minds. We try to move them from stasis to action, from buying from our competitor to buying from us. Too often, salespeople race ahead and try to change a client's mind without first understanding and respecting that person's views and opinions.

When you are truly caring, you build a connection and work from the customer's point of view. To illustrate, imagine yourself as the buyer. Would you want someone to try to change your mind without first taking the time to understand what you believe and why you believe it? Would you want someone to dismiss your interpretation of what is real and important? Or would you prefer to work with someone who "gets it" first and only then presents solutions?

4. Make Caring an Action.

Caring is not just an intellectual exercise; it's an action. There are countless ways to put caring into action. You can be present at your client's facility on a regular basis. Follow up. Offer new ideas that produce even greater results. Introduce your clients to other people who can use their services. Get your team together with their team to develop ways to work together more effectively. And that's just a short list—very short.

The list that you need to make here is the list of things that you need to do, right now, with your clients and your dream clients. To get you started, consider the following steps. Call the customer you haven't spoken to in months and that you know doesn't need to buy anything from you right now just to check on them personally. Send a thank-you card for no reason other than that you are grateful. Make a call to a client to present the résumé of another client's family member who is looking for work and who would be a great addition to their team.

5. Remember the Little Things.

After you receive an order, do you send a thank-you card? And do you thank all the people who helped you, from target to close? Or do you move on and forget about the client once she places her order?

When the order has been delivered, do you call and follow up? Do you make sure your client achieves the desired outcome? If a client struggles with what you have sold him, do you find out about it and do something? Or do you just hope someone else takes care of any problems that arise?

Saying thank you and following up may not seem like big things, but when it comes to proving that you care, little things loom large.

Visit www.theonlysalesguide.com *to download a work sheet to help you transform caring into action.*

Caring Is Cost Free

There is no conflict between selling to and caring about your customer. In fact, it's just the opposite. The more you care, the more effective you are as a salesperson.

The power of caring is unmatched, both inside and outside of your company. It's the foundation of trust, and it produces positive results. Those who care deeply about their clients—and who cultivate client relationships—will stand out from the crowd and be welcomed as trusted, valued partners.

FIRST MOVE—DO THIS NOW!

You already have clients and prospects. If you're like most of us, you haven't been proactive enough about maintaining those relationships. Make a list of three clients or prospects and call them simply to see how they are doing personally and professionally. Don't pitch them, and don't ask them for anything. Just call because you care.

RECOMMENDED READING

Green, Charles H. *Trust-Based Selling: Using Customer Focus and Collaboration to Build Long-Term Relationships*. New York: McGraw-Hill Education, 2005.

Peters, Tom. *The Little Big Things: 163 Ways to Pursue Excellence*. New York: Harper-Studio, 2010.

Sanders, Tim. *Love Is the Killer App: How to Win Business and Influence Friends*. New York: Crown Business, 2002.

Chapter 4

COMPETITIVENESS: A BURNING DESIRE TO BE THE BEST

Focus on being an invaluable resource to your prospects and clients. It's your only sustainable competitive advantage.

—Jill Konrath, author of *Agile Selling*

WE SALESPEOPLE ARE COMPETITIVE, OFTEN VERY MUCH SO. WE want to get our dream clients to sign on the dotted line. We also want to beat other salespeople to the punch, this time and every time. Don't you double your efforts when you know that your dream client has already met with your fiercest and most dangerous competitor? Doesn't the hair on the back of your neck stand up when you walk out of a presentation and find a competitor waiting in the lobby?

Having a competitive spirit is essential to sales success. And this drive to win can be very positive, motivating sales pros to serve customers in bigger and better ways, thereby creating more and more value.

THE COMPETITIVE SPECTRUM: FINDING THE STRONG SPOT

Unfortunately, we've all seen what happens when competition is pushed to the extreme. Witness the highly publicized humiliation of bicyclist Lance Armstrong, who ultimately admitted to cheating in cycling races. Or the firing of Indiana University basketball coach Bobby Knight, whose hypercompetitive behavior became abusive.

Intemperate, misdirected competitiveness can be harmful to a sales career. It can lead to immoral and illegal practices, such as offering bribes and kickbacks and price-fixing. And if we make customers the target of our competitiveness, we can poison our ability to create collaborative business relationships. This is hypercompetition, or competition run amok.

At the other end of the spectrum is what I call weak competition, which is trying to win by belittling other salespeople or their offerings or misrepresenting what you sell. Those with a weak competitive spirit don't try to improve themselves. Instead, they attempt to "win" by tearing down others or bamboozling potential clients. This is just as bad as hypercompetition.

Trying to win by making your competition look bad may work once or twice, but it is not an effective long-term strategy. That's because your focus is always on other salespeople and never on yourself. When you adopt a weak strategy, you actually become weaker yourself, for sabotaging your competitors and fooling your clients distracts you from the real work you must do to become a true competitor.

A true competitor is what I call the "strong competitor," the person who strives to win by becoming her absolute best. She primarily competes with herself. She focuses on her own improvement—what other salespeople do is secondary.

Instead of tearing down your competitors or pulling the wool over your customers' eyes, focus on improving yourself and on increasing the value you create for your clients. Then you'll move to the center of the competition spectrum, the place of power. As a strong competitor, you win by creating a high level of value for your clients. The strong competitor has a well-developed sense of honor, sportsmanship, and fair play. He is willing to fight hard and to do what is necessary to win—knowing that what's necessary is improving himself and offering genuine value. Every salesperson should aim for this sweet spot on the competitive spectrum.

SALES AS A ZERO-SUM GAME

In recent years, salespeople have been told that we should be more collaborative and cooperative. We've been informed that sales is not a zero-sum game, in which one side wins and the other loses. We've been told that there is plenty to go around.

Yet, sales is almost *always* a zero-sum game: one salesperson wins the customer's business, while all the others lose. For you to win a prospective customer's business, all of your competitors must lose. You need to be better than you were yesterday and better than your competitor is today.

Sales is a game with fixed boundaries. Most markets have limited playing space. When markets are mature, with fixed numbers of customers, or are stagnant or shrinking, winning often demands that you take your competitors' customers away from them. You may not like this, but remember, your competitors are always trying to do the same thing to you. You're both playing the same game. While you're calling their existing clients, they are searching for a chink in your armor, some way they can lure away your clients. This is the nature of sales.

To win under such conditions, you must become competitive. You must be at your absolute best and provide the highest possible value to your prospective customers. Your competitors are smart, aggressive, excellent salespeople, all of whom have the ability to create value. You need to respect their power. Otherwise, you might be lulled into a false sense of security, believing that your clients will stay true to you no matter how little you do for them.

YOUR COMPETITIVE NATURE IS VALUED

You already know that your company values your competitiveness—after all, it's a job requirement. The company itself is engaged in a struggle to capture new clients, grow revenue, increase profits, and expand its market share. It needs someone with a competitive spirit to achieve these goals—someone like you.

What you might not realize is how much your customers value your competitiveness. Many of them are engaged in a zero-sum game of their own, and they want to work with competitive salespeople who can help *them* compete more effectively. Your clients are not looking for a vendor. They want a partner who will charge into battle and tip the balance in their favor. They want a winner.

Society also values your competitiveness. As you compete for business, you work to create greater value for your clients and help them produce better results. The competition to create value brings new ideas, new solutions, and positive results. Healthy competition drives the upward spiral of innovation, progress, and growth.

THE ELEMENTS OF COMPETITION

Boxers fight for twelve tough rounds. They fight with everything they've got, pouring their hearts into their work. They are fueled by a burning desire to win. They pummel each other as hard as they can—and then they hug each other. They respect their opponents' hearts and spirits. They honor their competitors by preparing for the contest, knowing that the battle is dangerous and will test their wills and their abilities. This is the heart of the strong competitor. Embrace it and build your competitive spirit.

To compete effectively, you must combine the following attributes:

- **Desire:** If you don't really want it, you can't win it. Desire gets you out on the field. Coupling desire with optimism creates the strong belief that you can win. A strong competitor wants to win so badly that she can "taste" it.

- **Heart:** Long-term success is the result of working hard over the long run. You need heart (persistence) to hang in there when you're faced with seemingly insurmountable obstacles. You need heart to win the war, even when you lose battle after battle. If desire gets you on the field, heart is what keeps you in the game when the going gets tough.
- **Action:** Simply wanting to win is not enough. Winning requires action. A competitor takes the actions that position him to win.

THREE WAYS TO IGNITE YOUR COMPETITIVE SPIRIT

Here's how to combine desire, heart, and action to create a strong competitive spirit:

1. Play Your Game.

Salespeople weaken themselves when they play their competitors' games, trying to compete where their competitors are strongest. Yes, it's important for you to discover how your competitors intend to win and where their strengths lie. But it's equally important that you be aware of where your own strengths lie and how you are most likely to win.

For example, if a competitor's business model is based on offering the lowest price, competing on price will not be a winning strategy for you. To win, you must shift your prospective customer's decision criteria toward your strengths—for example, your superior product and the superior outcome you will produce, both of which are enabled by your higher price. This is *your* game, and even if it is more difficult to play, your odds of winning it increase.

Sometimes your competitor's strength lies in size and scale. For example, a major international company can serve its clients' needs across large geographic areas. If you are a smaller, "boutique" company, you can't compete in size and scale, so don't try. However, if your company happens to be geographically close to your prospect, your local presence can give you a competitive edge. Emphasize that you offer a greater presence at your client's site. Being small and nimble may also be advantageous, because your company can customize products, services, record keeping processes, and other interactions, giving your clients greater control. Your company's flat management structure—no multitiered bureaucracy to hold up approvals—also offers quick access to management and faster decisions when pressing needs arise. If massive size and scale aren't your game, be the agile competitor with fire in her belly and the ability to punch three divisions above her weight class.

Compete to win by playing *your* game, not your competitor's. Here's how:

- **Identify your company's overall business strategy.** Do you compete by having the lowest price, best product, or best overall solution? If you need help understanding these business strategies, I recommend that you read *The Discipline of Market Leaders: Choose Your Customers, Narrow Your Focus, Dominate Your Market* by Michael Treacy and Fred Wiersema.
- **Know your competitors.** What is their business model? What's their game? Will their larger size dominate their game plan? Or will they play up their range of products or services? Their price or their proximity? Something else?
- **Stick with your own strengths and don't compete where your competitor is strong.** If your competitor sells on price, how do you shift your client's decision criteria to the better results produced by your superior product? If your competitor has a stronger product, how do you shift your client's criteria to the better results you produce by having the best total solution?

Play your game strategically by shifting the competition to areas where you are strong and your competitor is weak.

For help with this, download a free work sheet at www.theonlysales guide.com.

2. Study Your Wins and Losses.

When you're a strong competitor, you take full responsibility for your losses. Instead of complaining that the competition didn't play fair or the client didn't understand what the other company was selling, you take personal responsibility for the outcome. In so doing, you empower yourself with the belief that you can improve and win next time.

During football season, each team plays a single game each week. Immediately after the game—win or lose—the players study the game films for lessons. Though you do not have game films to guide you, you do have a memory, as well as a record of all of your sales interactions. When you lose a sale to a competitor, ask yourself the following questions:

- What could I have done earlier in the sales process to improve my odds of winning?
- How would I change my sales process if I could do it all over again? My approach? My solutions? My pitch?
- What did my competitor do differently that provided him with the winning edge? What can I learn from his approach?

As painful as it can be to own your loss, it is powerful because it helps you improve. That is why strong competitors always ask themselves these questions.

You should also study your wins, asking yourself a different set of questions:

- Which strategy allowed me to win my prospect's business? How can I apply that same strategy to future deals?
- What did I do during my sales process that positioned me for a win?

Should I make this a permanent part of my process? Or should it only be used in certain cases?
- What made it easy for my prospect to say yes? What were the competitive differences that guided that decision?
- What was different this time, compared with the times I lost? How do I repeat what I've learned?

If you know how you lose, you can work to avoid repeating mistakes. And if you know how you win, you have a recipe you can follow in future deals.

3. Leave No Weapon Unfired.

Being a strong competitor with a burning desire to win means giving it all you've got, each and every time. You never leave a competitive situation saying, "I could have won, if only I had done X."

Here are three sometimes-overlooked weapons that can seal a win:

- **Think widely about the weapons you have available to you.** Sometimes winning requires proving that you and your company are committed to producing certain results. To demonstrate your level of commitment, bring a member of your management team on the sales call—but not just anyone. Ask the best person (perhaps it's your sales manager or someone in executive management) to go with you and present the case. Pull out all the stops.
- **Be willing to iterate.** Sometimes the difference between winning and losing means modifying your proposal. Rework it as much as necessary and ask for the opportunity to present it again. Fire this weapon.
- **Muster up proof providers.** Sometimes you need to demonstrate a track record of successes to earn new business. Consider asking your existing clients to call your prospective client and testify on your behalf. Even better, invite both to lunch and ask your existing client

to share all of the ways in which hiring you turned out to be a great decision. Pull that trigger.

Identify the weapons that are available to you and figure out how you can best use them to win. You've got them; don't be afraid to use them!

Be a Strong Competitor First, Last, and Always

Respect your competitors and believe that they are every bit as good as you are. Develop your competitive spirit, combining desire, heart, and action. Learn your competitors' strengths while playing to your own strengths as much as possible. Study your wins and losses for guidance in future competitions. Leave no weapon unfired. By following these guidelines, you'll become a strong competitor and a force to be reckoned with.

Competitiveness is not simply wanting to win. Everybody wants that. Wanting to win is a lot like hoping to win. It isn't action-oriented. *Wanting* doesn't mean that you'll move heaven and earth to win the deal. Competitiveness borders on *having* to win. Even the most competitive salesperson won't win every deal. But she'll try like hell—and keep trying.

FIRST MOVE—DO THIS NOW!

Look at your existing pipeline of opportunities. Identify the potential deals that you are working on where you have been too passive in competing for their business. Make a list of the one or two things you need to do now to compete for their business in a way that would demonstrate your desire and commitment to create more value than anyone else and earn their business.

RECOMMENDED READING

Cardone, Grant. *If You're Not First, You're Last: Sales Strategies to Dominate Your Market and Beat Your Competition*. Hoboken, NJ: Wiley, 2010.

Treacy, Michael, and Fred Wiersema. *The Discipline of Market Leaders: Choose Your Customers, Narrow Your Focus, Dominate Your Market*. New York: Basic Books, 2007.

Welch, Jack, and Suzy Welch. *Winning: The Ultimate Business How-To Book*. New York: HarperCollins, 2009.

Chapter 5

RESOURCEFULNESS: FINDING A WAY OR MAKING ONE

You don't have to search for inspiration if you get better at letting it find you.

—Don "the Idea Guy" Snyder, author of *100-WHATS of CREATIVITY*

I ONCE SAW A PICTURE OF THE FRONT WHEEL OF A CAR LOCKED into one of those parking boots designed to keep the car from moving until the driver pays a fine. It was *just* the front right wheel and the boot— the car was gone.

I knew there was no way to remove a locked boot from a wheel or remove the wheel from the car, since the boot covers the lug nuts. Or, at least, I *thought* I knew that. Yet somehow, someone had managed to remove the booted wheel from the car. It was a stunning example of resourcefulness. Whereas you and I might have seen a problem that could only be solved by paying a fine, that person saw a temporary setback that could be overcome by thinking about it in a new way.

RESOURCEFULNESS LEADS TO SALES SUCCESS

You'll undoubtedly face countless obstacles on your way to closing a sale. But being resourceful can allow you to find paths over, under, around, or through just about every obstacle. Meanwhile, your clients have their own challenges and expect you to help find ways around them. This makes successful selling an exercise in problem solving that requires resourcefulness.

Being resourceful means using your imagination, experience, and knowledge to solve a difficult problem. Resourcefulness is necessary at all stages of the sales process. To begin with, you have to be resourceful even to secure an appointment with your dream client. Your contacts at these companies get calls from dozens of salespeople, so you need ideas that allow you to differentiate yourself from your competitors and prove that you're a value creator. The more resourceful you are in generating new ideas and approaches that create value for your prospects, the more successful you will be in getting appointments.

One guy I know won a huge sales contest by sending a single shoe to a prospect with a note saying, "I just want to get my foot in the door." I've seen other salespeople send a remote-control car or plane to a prospect—without the remote. In order to get it, the prospect had to agree to a meeting. These are certainly gimmicky approaches, but they got attention because they were unique and the salespeople who dreamed them up were resourceful.

Once you make contact and begin to do your discovery, you may realize that it won't be easy to deliver what your prospect wants. This is a given: if your dream client's problems were easy to solve, another supplier would already have handled them. You must have superior solutions to these problems, which means being resourceful.

Your resourcefulness may win over one key prospect. But even after you've devised a solution, you may run into another obstacle: you're not just selling to one person or one department. More and more companies make decisions by consensus, with several departments weighing in. Some may like your solution while others do not. You may need to come up with new solutions that are acceptable to everyone so that a consensus can be reached.

RESOURCEFULNESS IS THE KEY TO RETENTION

Even after the sale has been made and your client is using your product or service, you must continue to be resourceful—for months, years, and decades. Your clients are continually hit with new challenges, opportunities, and conditions that require them to produce new results. You probably won the account in the first place because the current provider wasn't solving their problems, and the client became dissatisfied enough to make a change. This same dissatisfaction can easily arise again, so you must always be vigilant and resourceful if you want to keep your clients.

I once had a client who was very happy with the service we provided until he acquired a new, gigantic customer of his own. This new customer was very demanding and often wanted things right *now*. In the past, my client had given us seventy-two hours' notice when placing orders; now, he could afford only twelve. This meant that I had to redesign our processes to serve my client's new needs or lose him as a client. It was an exercise in resourcefulness, and it wasn't easy.

Resourcefulness must be part of how you approach every part of the sales process. Let me give you a couple examples.

Prospecting: I have seen salespeople send a custom video introducing themselves and their teams. I have seen salespeople send a remote-control car without the remote, offering to bring it to the customer. I have seen salespeople offer to share ideas that the customer hadn't yet been aware of to secure an appointment.

Presentation. I once had every employee who would be working for the client show up to the final presentation wearing signs that said **CHOOSE US!** to demonstrate their commitment to the client. This was an idea from one of the salespeople working for me—and it worked. We beat the largest firm in the world in our space for that deal.

To retain your clients, demonstrate your resourcefulness at every opportunity—that's a surefire way to create new value. At the end of the quarter, meet with your clients to propose a new idea or some change to your service that will lead to better results. Whenever you spend time with your clients—and you should spend as much time with them as possible—you will probably come up with ideas for making positive changes. And you'll have conversations with them that inform you about their ever-changing needs, a constant and never-ending source of future problems that demand your resourcefulness.

RESOURCEFULNESS IS ABOUT IDEAS AND SOLUTIONS

Resourceful salespeople can accomplish things that seem impossible because they approach problems with a different mind-set than do their less resourceful counterparts. They visualize ways that something might be achieved, identify alternative solutions, and generate new ideas as a matter of course. They put their creativity to work on behalf of their companies, their clients, and themselves.

I once had a prospective client whose employees were stealing time. A group of employees would show up late or leave work early while another employee punched the clock at the proper time for all of them. Competing firms tried to solve the problem in conventional ways: seeking to catch the employees in the act, hiring a guard to monitor the time clock, and so on. But these ideas proved ineffective and costly. My team decided to focus on the time clock itself. We found a small manufacturer of time clocks that incorporated a biometric hand scanner normally used in high-security facilities. The clocks were pricey, but the onetime expense was far more cost-effective than the ongoing theft of time. This resourceful solution won their business.

You now know that it's essential to be resourceful. But how do you do that? Let's look at the two component parts of resourcefulness:

- **Belief:** To be resourceful, you must abandon the self-defeating belief that something is impossible. Instead, embrace the empowering belief that you can *always* find a way. Resourceful people know that even though a solution may not be immediately obvious, it probably exists. In fact, possible solutions may already lie within your grasp. One of my clients had a problem with a product they manufactured, a small part of a door installation that was instrumental in keeping out water and light. Their patent was their competitive advantage. But it had expired, so something new was needed. The head of the design unit mistakenly believed that the new product had to keep passing a government-mandated test 100 percent of the time, when it actually had to pass just once to be certified. But believing that it was necessary—and *possible*—to invent such an amazingly reliable product, the designer did it. He believed that perfection was possible and saw the problem in a new way. He ended up creating the best product ever seen on the market in their space.
- **Imagination:** Sir Ken Robinson, author, speaker, and international adviser on education, describes imagination as "the ability to bring to mind things that are not present to our senses." Imagination helps you generate new ideas, whether entirely new or pieced together from other ideas. New ideas allow you to solve problems and create opportunities.

IF YOU KNOW EVERYTHING ALREADY, YOU CAN'T LEARN ANYTHING

Constantly coming up with new ideas and approaches is challenging. To do it, you might need to liberate yourself from past experiences by pushing them out of your consciousness. The ideal way to do this is to practice *shoshin*, a concept from Zen Buddhism that means "beginner's mind." When you look at something with a beginner's mind, you abandon your preconceptions, biases, past experiences, and other mental barriers that color the ways you perceive it. Instead, you see it with fresh eyes and an open mind. Often, this is the key to developing new ideas and finding new ways to solve problems.

Bruce Lee (yes, *that* Bruce Lee) told the story of a university professor who sought out a master to help him study Zen Buddhism. When the professor arrived, the Zen master offered him a cup of tea, which the professor graciously accepted. As they spoke, the Zen master continued to pour tea into the professor's cup until it overflowed. The professor said, "Sorry, but the cup is overflowing." The Zen master replied, "Oh, you noticed. To fit in any more, you must first empty your cup."

Sales veterans can have a similar problem. If you have come to believe there are certain ways to do things or if you stick too rigidly to what has worked in the past, your experience will interfere with your resourcefulness. To avoid this, adopt a beginner's mind and question whether your answers from the past are still the best answers for the future. Ask yourself the following questions:

- If I was looking at this problem for the first time, what are the four or five ways I might explore trying to produce a better result?
- How are other people solving this problem? What part of me is uncomfortable trying something new, and why does it make me uncomfortable?
- What has changed during the time I have been doing this the one way I have chosen? Is this still the right choice?

It's difficult to let go of your experiences and beliefs. Try acting as if you didn't already know the answer. Suddenly, you have to explore possibilities and generate ideas. And you have to believe that it is possible to find an answer—or perhaps several.

FIVE WAYS YOU CAN BE MORE RESOURCEFUL NOW

You are a deep and endless well of value-creating ideas. (Or you will be after you finish this chapter!) Let's work on ways to develop your resourcefulness:

1. Spend Time Thinking.

Seriously. You need to spend more time thinking, even though it is among the most difficult work you will ever do. Most people are more resourceful than they allow themselves to believe. While they have the ability to generate new, value-creating ideas, they don't exercise it often enough.

Make a commitment to, and schedule time for, thinking. Start by setting aside an hour a week just for thinking. If you don't know where to start, try asking yourself questions. What are some new things I might try to solve the problem this client is having now? Answering this question can help you generate possibilities. Why do all of my dream clients have this challenge right now? This question may help you discover an underlying systemic challenge and the solution.

Since this probably isn't something you practice often enough, you may be surprised at how hard it is to just sit and think about your customers and how you can help them in new ways. It can be tough to get started, but that difficulty will pass once you get your brain moving.

2. Generate Ideas.

Come up with lots of ideas—dozens of them. Do not try to develop "perfect" ideas, and don't worry if they seem difficult or improbable. Just generate them. Write down whatever comes to mind.

What has your attention is what most needs your attention. When you start writing, some idea or theme will present itself. You have to trust the process. If you need a little help getting started, it might be useful to ask yourself questions such as the following:

- What can I do to help my customers get better results?
- How can I fire up that stalled opportunity? What haven't I tried yet?
- What are the most common problems my clients face? What new solutions can I suggest?

Write out, in detail, your answers to the preceding questions. When you've filled up three pages of a legal pad, I promise you there will be something there worth pursuing.

The ability to solve problems in new ways is not limited to a few geniuses. We were born with the ability to imagine and create. You've seen the way children play naturally, deep in self-created worlds and situations. It's the "adult" mind-set that gets in the way of using imagination, creativity, and resourcefulness. You can bypass the adult mind-set just by sitting and thinking and then writing down whatever comes to mind.

3. Explore Ideas without Judgment.

Some people are not as resourceful as they could be because they are too judgmental. When they hear a new idea or develop one of their own, they instantly think of all the reasons it will fail. Their favorite saying is, "We tried that once, and it didn't work." And maybe it won't—but maybe it can be modified until it does work. Or maybe it only works after you get a little better at executing the idea.

If you try to imagine and create while simultaneously judging what you come up with, the critical part of your mind will shut down the creative part. So when you are trying to be more resourceful, focus solely on generating ideas. Save the judging, sorting, and ranking of ideas for later. Let someone else play devil's advocate. Your job is to play angel's advocate.

4. Identify Alternatives.

It is easy to believe that when you're after a certain outcome, you must work your tail off to obtain it. Then you must keep at it, even when you're producing the desired results.

Dogged determination is admirable, but often there's a better approach. My friend Don Snyder, author of *100-WHATS of CREATIVITY* and a master of creativity, likes to say, "Asking better questions will get you better answers."

In this case, the better question might be, "What are *all* my choices of action—not just this one that's working?"

For example, suppose you need a better pipeline of opportunities. You might decide that you need to make more cold calls, which has worked for you in the past. But that might not be enough. So, what other choices are available? You might consider referrals, networking, trade shows, or even things like Webinars that could generate leads. Then there are less obvious approaches, such as sending your dream client a trash can with your brochures already in it, an idea that Don "the Idea Guy" Snyder sold to Jeffrey Gitomer.

Give yourself lots of options and explore them all. You may find something that works better than what you're currently doing or that a combination of several techniques produces the best result.

5. Stay Positive.

If you want to ruin your career in sales, just start saying, "It can't be done." Say it to your clients, say it to yourself, and you're on your way out of the business.

This simple sentence is a guaranteed sales killer for two reasons. First, when you say "It can't be done," you disempower yourself. If you believe that something can't be done—which means, by extension, that *you* can't do it—why even bother to try? Tell yourself that scheduling an appointment with a dream client can't be done because that customer is already working with a competitor, and you have just given yourself a reason not to try. The resourceful salesperson, on the other hand, looks at that same situation and thinks, "I know there are ways into this company, but what are they? What else can I try? How can I use my belief, research, and imagination to get an appointment and make the sale?"

Second, to say "It can't be done" is to avoid personal accountability. If you truly cannot do something, then you also can't be held responsible for it. You absolve yourself of the responsibility to attempt it (and of responsibility for the outcome) by saying—and believing—that it can't be done. But you, as a salesperson, have been hired to find a way, and your customers expect you to help them. The only way to meet these expectations is to eradicate "it can't be done" from your vocabulary and put your resourcefulness to work.

In truth, you *can* find a way. Further, you need to do so before some other resourceful salesperson comes up with an idea and beats you to the punch.

Resourcefulness is one of your most powerful sales weapons. Your creativity gives you the ability to solve problems and overcome challenges. Exercising your resourcefulness requires that you look at problems differently and ask different questions. This is the heart of innovation and improvement, and it is your best shot at helping clients and companies produce better results.

The Resourceful Salesperson Reaps the Rewards

A lack of resourcefulness leads to complacency, which leads to client dissatisfaction, which leads to your replacement by a competitor. The resourceful salesperson always looks for new and imaginative ways to help customers improve their results and, in doing so, becomes more likely to win and keep clients.

Great salespeople are resourceful. They use their resourcefulness to find ways into prospects that others fail to discover. Once inside, they work with their prospects to generate ideas that create a vision of how a problem may be solved or a competitive advantage might be gained—for them and for their dream client.

FIRST MOVE—DO THIS NOW!

Resourcefulness is the application of imagination and creativity to some problem or challenge. What's the one problem you are struggling with now that, if overcome, would allow you to create some breakthrough result? Sit down with a pen and paper and make a list of no less than five things that you could do to produce the result you need. You can come up with five, but if you need more ideas, enlist the help of someone from outside your industry who can look at the problem without being constrained by working in your field.

RECOMMENDED READING

Foster, Jack. *How to Get Ideas*. San Francisco: Berrett-Koehler Publishers, 2007.

Sanders, Tim. *Dealstorming: The Secret Weapon That Can Solve Your Toughest Sales Challenges*. New York: Portfolio, 2016.

Snyder, Don "the Idea Guy." *100-Whats of Creativity*. www.100whatsbook.com, 2009.

Von Oech, Roger. *A Whack on the Side of the Head: How You Can Be More Creative*. Menlo Park, CA: Creative Think, 2011.

Chapter 6

INITIATIVE: TAKING ACTION BEFORE IT IS NECESSARY

Being prepared is critically important but without focused, massive action all the preparation in the world won't help you succeed.

—Hector LaMarque, legendary sales leader of Primerica

YOU ARE UNDOUBTEDLY A GREAT LEAPER. WHEN AN EXISTING OR prospective customer says, "Jump!" you smile and ask, "How high?"

While it's great to be responsive to your clients' needs, succeeding in sales requires more than that. You need to anticipate your clients' needs instead of waiting for them to tell you what they want. Instead of them telling you to jump, you want your surprised clients to see you jumping of your own accord.

You can't succeed in sales (or anything else) just by waiting. You can't expect your dream clients to raise their hands, ring your phone, or send you an e-mail requesting help. They already have plenty of passive, reactive people in their lives. You need to take the initiative, define yourself, and differentiate your offering.

PHYSICS ON YOUR SIDE

Newton's first law of motion says that an object at rest tends to remain at rest, and an object in motion remains in motion—unless either is acted upon by an external force. In other words, objects tend to keep on doing what they're doing. You can become your own force and put yourself in motion just by taking the initiative. And once you're moving toward success, you'll find that it's easy to stay that way. It's called momentum, the "big mo," and it is a game changer.

Your dream clients are also likely to continue doing what they're currently doing. They may want something better but will probably continue in their current direction unless *you* become an external force acting on them. Start taking positive actions now!

SALES IS ALL ABOUT *ACTION*

Sales is an action-oriented endeavor, so waiting can be considered anathema. For the successful salesperson, there is no such thing as waiting for any of the following:

- **Opportunities.** Staring at your phone, hoping that prospects will return your calls or e-mails, is a recipe for disaster. Your dream clients are too busy to return calls from salespeople, many of whom waste their time. If these clients are in need of help, they typically need to wait only an hour or two before they are contacted by your initiative-taking competitor. Here's a hard truth: Opportunities don't land in your lap. It's up to you to take the initiative and create them.
- **Someone else.** It's a poor strategy to wait for marketing to develop and provide you with leads. Leads are the icing on the cake, not the cake itself. You can't wait for anyone to do your work for you, even if what they do is supposed to help you. Seize the initiative and develop your own opportunity pipeline.

- **Your dream clients to become dissatisfied.** Waiting for a dream client to ask you for help is a reactive and passive strategy. You've already made hundreds, perhaps thousands, of sales calls. You understand your industry and know what's needed. Rather than waiting to be asked, offer your dream clients new information and ideas. Taking the initiative makes you powerful and separates you from the crowd.

- **Your dream clients to reach consensus.** Your opportunities will die a certain death if you wait around for clients and prospects to build a consensus for change—and for your solution—within their organizations. If they could develop such support without you, they would have done it already. The status quo will wait you out, like it has so many salespeople before you—unless you take action to change it.

- **Your dream clients to lead.** Waiting for your clients to tell you how to roll out your solution is passive. In many cases, they don't know how to implement your services. While you're standing around waiting for them to lead, they're waiting for the same thing from you. What is your implementation plan? Develop and present it before you're asked.

Remember, while you are waiting around for things to happen, your dream clients are waiting for action from some caring, resourceful value creator. They're waiting for someone who can really help them, for someone to share the big, value-creating idea that will produce the results they desperately need. Your dream clients are waiting for someone to be proactive and take the initiative.

If you're waiting . . . and they're waiting . . . what's going to happen? Nothing. And then someone else will swoop in and steal your client right from under your nose.

DON'T WAIT. INITIATE!

Set yourself in motion and seize the initiative. Be proactive, engaged, and innovative:

- **Proactive:** Act before others even realize that action is needed. Scout out opportunities for improvement and problems that need to be addressed. Then be there first, with solutions.
- **Engaged:** Become fully engaged in your work, think deeply, and discover opportunities that benefit your customers, your company, and yourself. Do more than is expected and do it now.
- **Innovative:** Find new, unusual ways to improve outcomes, even if your current techniques are working.

One saleswoman I know sells a very complex solution that requires her company to use partner businesses to collect information from new clients. The data quality often turns out to be very poor, but the defects remain hidden until her new clients discover they cannot achieve the outcomes they need and have paid for.

Eager to be proactive, this saleswoman now acts early to review the data collection process and head off problems. She meets with her client and reviews the information to ensure that it is 100 percent correct. Such action is usually beyond the jurisdiction of the sales department, but her approach to these challenges has made her something more than a salesperson to her client—she is now a trusted adviser. Taking initiative can redefine the way your dream clients perceive you and markedly increase the value you bring.

CUSTOMERS VALUE INITIATIVE

Your dream clients want you to be two steps ahead of them, already doing what needs to be done next without being asked. They want you to act like a member of their management team, using your responsiveness on their behalf.

For decades, we have been taught that good salespeople diagnose before they prescribe. But how does that square with what you hear from your customers? When I meet with executives, I rarely hear them say, "Help us diagnose our problems." What they usually say is, "Look, we don't know what we don't know. You are on the outside; you see what other companies are doing. What should we do next?" My customers want me to provide them with new ideas. Initiative opens sales opportunities. The skills of diagnosis and prescription are deployed after that.

The most successful salespeople constantly bring new ideas to their customers. They proactively deliver the next new thing that has the potential to propel their customers' businesses to new heights. Their initiative drives their customers' results.

FEAR COMPLACENCY

Think about the last customer you lost. You felt abandoned, didn't you? You had a great relationship, you did good work together, and you delivered everything you promised. Over time, you had less to do to maintain the relationship, so you did less. Who really abandoned whom? As Jill Griffin, author of *Customer Loyalty: How to Earn It, How to Keep It*, points out, more clients are lost due to benign neglect than for any other problem.

It's easy to become complacent. We work hard to win a customer, sign a contract, and build a strong relationship. But then we're lulled into the comfortable yet false belief that we own the account and always will. We move on to invest our energy elsewhere, neglecting that customer's needs. We stop calling and visiting. We don't realize that the customer is struggling with unresolved problems. In the meantime, another salesperson takes initiative to solve the customer's current challenges—and the account you thought was locked down is lost when your customer goes with a competitor.

The antidote to complacency is initiative. Initiative is irrefutable evidence that you care about your customers, their challenges, and their business results. It protects you from customer defections by ensuring that you continually bring them new ideas and deliver improved results. In short, you create customer value on a continual basis. When you finish implementing one new idea, immediately start making the case for the next one.

Remember: absence doesn't make the heart grow fonder; absence makes the heart go wander. When you stop taking initiative, you drive your clients straight into the arms of your competitor. Again, the same dissatisfaction that created an opportunity for you to win this client does the same for that competitor. That's why it is critical to act proactively—to seek out new ways to create value for your client. It will ward off competitive threats.

HOW TO TAKE INITIATIVE

Initiative is not something to be trotted out only when things get rocky. It needs to be part of your daily routine, a repeated and repeatable process.

To take initiative, you first need ideas and insights that you can act upon. There are three major sources of ideas and insights:

1. Get Ideas from Your Team.

Schedule a monthly meeting with your sales team and develop fresh perspectives on how to create value for your clients. Discuss the common challenges that your customers face and share solutions that have produced the best results. Then go further and brainstorm ideas that, if implemented, could create even greater value for your clients. There's an excellent chance that the ideas you need already live within your company's walls—you just have to take the initiative to draw them out and put them into practice.

In my family's staffing business, we had a problem with employees who didn't show up for work once we placed them. During a staff meeting, someone mentioned that new hires who came to our office to get the details of their assignments showed up for work at higher rates than those who did not. We decided to make it mandatory for each individual to receive his or her assignment in a face-to-face meeting, even though it took longer and was more expensive for our business. The results were undeniable: our show-up rate skyrocketed.

2. Build on Your Experience.

Once you've worked with clients in a particular industry, you know the processes; you know how they do things, and you understand how they implement the solutions you sell. Now take a look at how other industries operate. Study the processes that work in a different industry and then apply them in yours.

When I started in the staffing industry, the document-management (copier) industry had employees on-site at customers' businesses to manage their copiers and paper. My staffing company adopted this idea and put employees on-site at our clients' locations. An idea from one industry was easily applied to a different industry. Now the idea of managed service on-site is commonplace.

This kind of insight creates value and changes your clients' results for the better. And this insight need not be a grand idea. You can routinely transfer smaller value-creating ideas to your customers and get very positive results.

3. Swim against the Industry Tide.

Ideas and insights can often come from simply analyzing your own industry and making a change. Identify a standard industry practice and explore how it could be done differently. Think about the things in your industry that elicit a comment such as, "We don't do that." Now ask yourself, "What if we *did* do that?" Or "*How* could we do that?"

One of my clients works in an industry in which his competitors sell at a low price but make up the margin by taking significant cuts from the vendors they use to serve their customers. My client decided to swim against the tide by refusing to take money from the vendors, choosing instead to be transparent. By explaining to his clients why he is more expensive and how this benefits them, he wins their trust—and their business.

Here's another example. Many hotels in major cities transport customers to and from the airport. One hotel that I often stay at decided that it wouldn't just take customers to the airport—it would shuttle them *any-where* they wanted to go. This requires extra drivers and extra costs, but the hotel is being proactive in serving its customers' needs. Other hotels said, "No, that's too expensive," but this one said, "Yes!" It may cost a little more, but it generates fierce loyalty.

Look for Everyday Opportunities and Challenges

One of my customers sells travel services, and she has a client who takes the same vacation every year. One year, she noticed that she could save her client more than 30 percent of the overall price by booking her vacation three months early. She called her client to share this opportunity. The client booked the vacation and was so pleased that she booked a second, more expensive holiday as well.

You have countless opportunities to exercise initiative every day. Your clients most likely place the same orders over and over, so you can anticipate their needs and be ready to meet them. They may also face the same challenges regularly. Help them out by providing them with a user guide or video that explains how to handle these problems. Take the initiative and provide the kinds of support you know your clients need.

You may also be able to anticipate political, legislative, economic, technological, and social changes that can affect your clients' businesses. Develop a reputation for helping clients see into the future by keeping them informed about upcoming changes and how these changes may impact business. By taking initiative, you will become the trusted adviser your customers count on to help prevent problems.

Proactively Share New Ideas and Insights

Build initiative into your process. Schedule quarterly meetings with clients to review your performance and relationships. These quarterly meetings are chances to gather all of the stakeholders in your customer's company. They will help you identify the changes you can make in order to provide better service. Your customers may also have their own ideas about how you can help them. By meeting every ninety days, you can continually make positive changes and receive feedback that informs your future actions. You can also take what you learn from one customer's quarterly business review and apply it to your other customers.

Start Jumping!

Your clients are always in need of new ideas and solutions because they are always under stress. Your competitors are probing for weaknesses in your relationships and trying to snatch away your business. Don't wait: act now!

Being proactive and taking initiative is how salespeople develop high-value, strategic relationships that create lifetime clients.

FIRST MOVE—DO THIS NOW!

Which of your clients have you been neglecting? (There is probably more than one.) Let's start with the most important client. What is the next initiative that you believe they should embark on now? Write a one-page business case for that initiative, and call that client to schedule a lunch meeting with them. During lunch, apologize for not bringing them this idea sooner, and ask for permission to pitch them the initiative that you know will help propel their business forward—and your relationship along with it.

RECOMMENDED READING

Covey, Stephen R., Roger A. Merrill, and Rebecca R. Merrill. *First Things First.* West Valley City, UT: Franklin Covey, 2015.

Chapter 7

PERSISTENCE: BREAKING THROUGH RESISTANCE

The single biggest difference between those who achieve their dreams and everyone else is their willingness to keep trying long after it seems logical, reasonable, fun, fair, or smart.

—Dan Waldschmidt, author of *EDGY Conversations*

TRUE STORY: I CALLED ONE OF MY DREAM CLIENTS WEEKLY FOR seventy-five weeks and left seventy-five voice-mail messages before he finally picked up his phone on week seventy-six. When I asked him for an appointment, he replied, exasperated, "You've called me a million times!" He was obviously unimpressed with my pigheaded, relentless pursuit of the opportunity to serve him.

"Actually," I replied lightly, "it's only *seventy-six*."

A moment passed before he said, "Well, it seemed like a million to me. If you come out right now, I'll give you an order."

Two minutes later, I was in my car. Twenty minutes after that, I was in his office, taking an order. Like magic, he had been transformed from a dream client to an actual client!

That's how persistence works. If you don't accept "no," don't give up, and don't bow to the status quo, a window of opportunity will eventually crack open and you will be standing in front of it. If it doesn't crack open, just keep prying it with a crowbar until it gives.

Persistence is the act of selecting a desired outcome and pursuing it *until you achieve it*. It is being resolute, patient, unshakable, and remaining doggedly on the trail of your goals. You want something badly, and you go after it. You never give up. I mean *never*.

Persistence, a critical element of sales success, is the determined pursuit of a goal when it's clear that it can't be easily achieved. It's the willingness to press on. Calvin Coolidge once said that nothing can take the place of persistence. He went on to clarify, saying, "Talent will not; nothing is more common than unsuccessful people with talent. Genius will not; unrewarded genius is almost a proverb. Education will not; the world is full of educated failures. Persistence and determination alone are omnipotent." "Omnipotent!" That's a powerful word, isn't it?

I'm sure you know people who are so sharp you could cut yourself on their intelligence, yet they perform poorly because they don't persist in their efforts. Certain of the people who graduated with me and earned the exact same degree as I did have never stuck with anything long enough to do well. They lacked nothing except persistence: the ability to keep hustling until you've made it over the goal line.

Persistence is made up of three major qualities:

- **Determination:** a firm—indeed, unshakable—intention to achieve a goal. You never, ever give up. You stay focused and committed to your goal, even when you fail and even when you don't know how you will ever succeed.
- **Tenacity:** the bulldog-like attribute of clamping down and holding on, no matter what. The word "dogged" is a good synonym for tenacity.
- **Grit:** a blend of courage and resolve that propels you forward despite obstacles and rejection. You aren't afraid to suck it up and tough it out—to get a little dirt on you.

REMEMBER THAT "NO" ONLY MEANS "NOT NOW"

"No" is the most common word in sales. Most of your potential customers will say no the first time you call. They'll say no to some of the commitments you need from them to move an opportunity forward. They'll say no at the end of your pitch, especially when it comes to your price. But if you give up whenever you hear the word "no," how long do you think it will be before you have no prospects left to call on? Most of them say no to your first attempt to secure a meeting!

Though it may be difficult at first, refuse to attach a negative meaning to the word "no." Don't believe it's a personal rejection that lessens your value as a human being. Instead, view it as feedback. "No" tells you to change your approach, create more value, or try again later. A "no" is not failure. It's information.

Even a "no" at the end of a hard-fought contest that resulted in a win for your competitor doesn't really mean no. Many of your prospects will not buy from you—sometimes because they've chosen your competitor, sometimes for other reasons. You identified an opportunity, competed for it, and lost. That doesn't mean you should step away; be persistent and stay engaged with customers no matter what. The successful salesperson knows the game is always on. A situation is only unrecoverable when *you* walk away, when *you* give up.

If you really want that prospect, don't give up. Regroup—and then nurture the relationship so you'll be in front when the next opportunity arises. Direct your efforts at winning the customer over the long term. And remember that your competitor is just as susceptible to complacency as everyone else is. This means that it's only a matter of time before he stumbles. When that happens, you'll be first in line to get your dream client's business.

Be persistent, stay engaged, and professionally persist, always ready to seize opportunities. These are key to winning a client's business, even in the face of "no."

BE PROFESSIONALLY PERSISTENT— NOT A NUISANCE

While it's important to keep showing up, offering ideas and information, don't harass your customers. A persistent salesperson elicits the admiration of the customer, even if it's sometimes a bit resigned. I've had clients tell me they were giving me an appointment only because I was so persistent. I've had others say that anyone as persistent as I am is worth having on their team. But there is a line between being persistent and being a nuisance, and it's one you should never cross.

The difference between being persistent and a nuisance lies in the content of your communication. If every communication is an obvious attempt to sell the customer, you quickly become a nuisance. If every communication includes value-producing information, you will be seen as persistent in a good way.

Remember that with every interaction, you define yourself as either a value creator or a time waster. Consider the widely used quarterly check-in calls that salespeople make on their prospective and current customers. I think they are a time-wasting nuisance, used by salespeople who have no value to offer.

There's one salesperson who has called me once a quarter for almost twenty years. Every call is exactly the same. He says, "This is Matt with [company name removed to spare it from horrifying embarrassment]. I just wanted to check in and see if anything has changed."

I always give him the same reply. "Nope. Nothing's changed."

Matt, undeterred, asks, "Can I call you again to check in next quarter to see if anything has changed?"

Has anything changed? Matt! In the last two decades, all *kinds* of things have changed—in my company, in my industry, in the economy . . . in the world! It would be impossible to miss the massive technological, economic, and cultural changes of the last twenty years. Yet Matt has not noticed anything noteworthy enough to ask how it has impacted my business. He has not shared a single idea as to how he can help me. This makes Matt a nuisance. I keep agreeing to take his calls because the value of this story as a lesson for salespeople grows with every passing year. But, alas, poor Matt has never gained my business.

If you call to ask your prospective client "if anything has changed," you will immediately identify yourself as a time waster. Instead of saying you're "checking in"—words that signal you have nothing of value to offer—create value by sharing ideas with your prospects *before* they become your customers. Develop the relationships you need now so that when the time comes to sell, the customer already sees you as a person with value-laden ideas and the ability to turn them into reality.

TIMING IS EVERYTHING

The secret to persistence is knowing when to wait patiently and when to strike. Once I identified a dream client, a company with needs that were a perfect match for our offerings. It was a no-brainer—except that the one executive with the authority to purchase refused to give me an opportunity to sell her. I pushed; she pushed back. I was unrelenting; she was unmoved. According to my records, this went on for over seven years. I jokingly said to my friends that she "would have to die" before I'd be given an opportunity to help this company. That wasn't quite true, though I couldn't get a foot in the door until she left the company.

The minute she left, I got on the phone with her replacement. How did I know her predecessor had left? I had called on her persistently during those seven years, constantly trying to create value even though I constantly heard "no." Then one day I was told, "She is no longer with the company." Within days, I met my obstacle's replacement, made the case that we were the right partner, and won a $2 million account with a massive firm with a nationally known brand name.

This is why you persist: so you will be in the right place at the right time. Since you won't know when the right time is, being a constant presence ensures that you're there when it's time to strike.

Sometimes you just have to wait out the roadblocks. Be patient and act with restraint, knowing that, at some point, things will turn in your favor. When they do, you'll be there, ready to act aggressively to capitalize on the opportunity.

THREE WAYS TO IMPROVE AND APPLY PERSISTENCE

Let's draw a line in the sand here. From this day forward, you will be a bulldog. No backing up or backing off, no giving up or giving in. You will persist in the pursuit of your goals, come hell or high water. You will be a gritty, determined, persistent, pigheaded value creator.

Are you ready to do some work to improve your persistence? Let's dig in.

1. Reframe Setbacks.

Setbacks and obstacles are simply a part of sales; there's no way to avoid them. To be successful in the long term, you must refrain from attaching negative meaning to them. Instead, reframe setbacks and obstacles as feedback that helps you make adjustments. Then try again.

The words you use in self-talk can help you see a "no" or a defeat in a positive light. Instead of saying to yourself, "I'll never get this client to see me," say, "I've just nurtured our budding relationship. A few more calls, and he'll give me the appointment." Rather than seeing a loss as a permanent defeat, say to yourself, "They just signed a one-year contract with my competitor. That means they have three hundred sixty-five days left before I win their business. I am so right for them!"

Selling is like solving a puzzle. When you get stuck, you try something new, become more resourceful, and persist until you find an approach that works. Some of the best clients you will ever have will be the most difficult to obtain. If you want to win them, you'll have to persist in solving that puzzle.

There's a side benefit to winning clients that are tough to win—they're tough for your competitors to win, too. Most of your competitors won't be as persistent as you are, making your tough dream-client account much safer over the long run.

2. Reset the Game Clock.

In basketball, the game is over when the buzzer sounds. There is no buzzer in sales . . . because the game never ends.

I can't tell you how often salespeople ask, "When can I quit calling on a prospect?" They are just waiting for the buzzer instead of driving down the court, trying to score. They want to give up because the prospect is difficult to win. But a no right now doesn't mean no forever. And why would you ever stop calling on your dream client, knowing that you can create more value than anyone else can?

I once heard Harvey Mackay, a revered motivational speaker and best-selling author of business books, speak about his first job in sales. He asked an old, grizzled sales veteran when it was OK to quit. The veteran replied, "When they die or you die." I've used this story dozens of times and in many speeches, and it always gets a laugh. It also empowers people to keep trying. As long as you have the ability to help your prospects produce better results, keep calling on them.

You may think a certain sales opportunity has been lost, but in truth, that game hasn't ended—it's just begun. Be persistent and take actions today that will help you win the customer in the future. Every time you fail to make a sale, move the hands of the game clock back to the beginning of play and start again. Better yet, banish all thoughts of a game-ending buzzer because the game is never over.

If you have not already done so, make a list of dream clients that you have competed for and lost. Let these be the accounts you compete for persistently, until they die or you die.

3. Try Something New.

Success is often a matter of experimentation—endless attempts to find the key that opens an opportunity. Thomas Edison tried more than three thousand different materials before he discovered a practical filament for the lightbulb. "If I find ten thousand ways something won't work, I haven't failed," he said. "I am not discouraged because every wrong attempt discarded is often a step forward." Edison may have exaggerated his number of failures, but the point he makes is powerful. He persisted. He knew that he would find a way eventually. You can do the same, and it won't require ten thousand attempts.

Think of an outcome you are trying to achieve and make a list of actions that can move you closer to your goal. Don't worry about how big and transformational or small and insignificant these actions may be. The key to being professionally persistent is to access an arsenal of tools, ideas, and techniques such as the following:

- When your dream client refuses your phone call requesting an appointment, send a white paper with a personal note telling how the paper's main idea might help her produce better results.
- When your dream client rejects your e-mailed request for an appointment, send a follow-up e-mail with a story about how you are helping a similar client.
- When you lose an opportunity, request a meeting to discover why the dream client chose your competitor. Afterward, be sure to say, "Thanks for the feedback!" and ask for the opportunity to try again. When you get that opportunity, make the changes necessary to win. And while you are waiting in the wings, persistently connect with your "lost" prospect by sharing your latest and greatest value-creating ideas.

You must continue to pursue the client's business over the long haul, if for no other reason than that's how he will get to know you—even if only distantly. I know some salespeople who never leave voice-mail messages when they prospect. This means that when they finally do get the prospect on the phone, he hears the salesperson's name and voice for the first time. The salesperson is a complete stranger instead of being known as a professionally persistent value creator. So leave that voice mail, but keep it short so your prospect will listen all the way to the end. Be sure he knows that you are pursuing him.

Make a list of all the actions you can take as well as all of the tools you have to support your professional persistence. Schedule these actions on your calendar. Then keep working this list, pausing only to review the outcomes of your actions, capture feedback, and make adjustments.

It's *Never* Over!

Persistence means that you hear "no" and continue pursuing an opportunity. It will keep you afloat and swimming in a career that Norman Hall, the last Fuller Brush man, characterized as "an ocean of rejection." Keep calling—for years if you have to—and never fail to nurture relationships, even when there is no indication that you will ever have a real shot at transforming that prospect into a customer. It's a surefire road to success. Never give up!

FIRST MOVE—DO THIS NOW!

We're going to have to go backward to go forward here. Generate a list of the deals that you lost in the last twelve months. How many of these prospective clients have you continued to pursue? If you're like most people, the answer is, "Not many." But if these prospects were worth pursuing then, they are worth pursuing now. Restart your prospecting effort by calling to reengage with each of these prospects by sharing a new value-creating idea or to schedule a meeting. Some of these

---

prospects are already unhappy they chose your competitor. They're waiting for you.

RECOMMENDED READING

Pink, Daniel H. *To Sell Is Human: The Surprising Truth about Moving Others.* New York: Riverhead, 2012.

Waldschmidt, Dan. *EDGY Conversations: How Ordinary People Can Achieve Outrageous Success.* South Jordan, UT: Next Century Publishing, 2014.

Chapter 8

COMMUNICATION: LISTENING AND CONNECTING

Trust is a relationship, and it begins with listening. Not data-driven, analytical listening, but the kind of listening that affirms to the customer that you "get" them and that they matter.

—**Charles H. Green, author of** *Trust-Based Selling*

TRUE STORY: A SALESPERSON ACTUALLY SAID TO A PROSPECTIVE client, "I need the deal to work this way because that is how I maximize my commission."

We call this "commission breath," a dangerous form of halitosis that literally melts your customer's face off—and costs you the deal. This salesman thought he was communicating that his intentions were pure, yet he communicated exactly the opposite. Or as George Bernard Shaw put it, "The single biggest problem in communication is the illusion that it has taken place."

COMMUNICATION IS NOT JUST PRESENTATION

Many salespeople believe that being good communicators means speaking well and persuasively conveying their ideas. In other words, they think that good presentation skills are the same thing as good communication. While being able to speak, present, and persuade does allow you to impart information, this is only part of the communication that takes place in every sales interaction—and it's often the least important part. The more important part is conveying the idea that you care about your customer and about solving her problem.

The key word here is "convey." You can say the words "I care" over and over again, but they just disappear into thin air. However, the ideas you convey need to demonstrate that you were listening and that you picked up your prospective client's wants and needs. What's the best way to convey information? Listen carefully to everything the other person has to say and then respond appropriately.

Salespeople often believe that communication is about pushing their own ideas. They operate as if communication flows in only one direction—from them to their prospects or existing clients—and that it's all about selling. For them, communication is more megaphone than telephone. However, simply sending "buy my product" information in one direction does not translate into effective selling. In fact, it's just the opposite; this kind of communication destroys the ability to sell. No one wants to buy from a walking, talking Web site that spews out information or rattles off endless lists of specs, features, and benefits.

Good communication stems from good listening; it is an extension of caring and facilitates sales. Stephen Covey got it right when he said, "Seek first to understand, and then to be understood." It is critical that you get these in the right order if you want to communicate well.

LISTEN TO THEM, NOT TO YOURSELF

Have you ever noticed your mind racing ahead while your prospect is speaking? Is the voice in your head sometimes louder than the voice of your client? I can't tell you how often this has happened to me. I had to work harder than a Buddhist monk to quiet my mind so I could listen without planning my responses—or worse, not even waiting to share my point but interrupting before the other person was finished. It's still not always easy to control myself, but I've found that I can learn a lot more by listening to others instead of to myself. As it turns out, I already know what I think. You know what you think, too.

To sell effectively, you need to listen effectively. Listen to the words your customers use to describe their situations, challenges, and opportunities. Also, listen carefully to what is *not* being said. Have you ever heard a prospect say "We're pretty happy" in a tone that was lackluster? The disconnect between his words and tone tells you what you really need to know. When you pay attention, you can pick up such incongruities, as well as other clues. Listen with the goal of understanding your clients' feelings, their dissatisfactions, hopes, dreams, and fears. It will do much to help you choose the most effective sales approaches.

Naturally, you can't listen to a client if you are focusing on that voice inside your head, the one reviewing the information and arguments that you're about to dump on the client. Listen to the client so you can gain understanding. Only then should you think about what you're going to say. Remember: no matter how polished you are as a presenter, your ability to communicate is made more powerful by listening first. Or as the great Steven Tyler of the band Aerosmith once sang, "Like the reason a dog / Has so many friends / He wags his tail instead of his tongue."

GOOD QUESTIONS ARE MORE POWERFUL THAN GREAT STATEMENTS

OK, let's assume that you've listened with attention and interest, and now it's time for you to speak. What do you say? Should you make your pitch? Probably not.

The most important tool for salespeople is a great set of questions to ask clients, coupled with the intention of fully understanding their needs by listening closely to their answers. (Yes, more listening!) Asking powerful questions demonstrates your business acumen and situational knowledge. Great questions can set you apart from your competitors and establish you as a subject expert, a trusted adviser, and a consultative salesperson. They will indicate that you are genuinely interested and help you gather necessary information. You know this from the times you've heard your dream client say, "That's a great question."

You can't learn anything about your clients' needs by talking about your product or solution. Neither can you learn your clients' preferences or decision-making processes. The most effective communication is a dialogue: you ask pertinent, thoughtful questions and listen carefully to the replies to gain real understanding. Only after you demonstrate that you truly understand the client's situation, feelings, and preferences can you effectively present your ideas and solutions as part of the continuing dialogue.

WHEN DO YOU "SELL"?

You may feel a strong temptation to rattle off the features of your product or service, run your scripts, and otherwise *sell, sell, sell.*

But hold back. Wait until you've conveyed interest in your client's situation, needs, and preferences and have established trust by listening and asking. Then you can present the information and ideas that show why your solution is the ideal one for the prospect or client, tying it back to the things she shared with you when she was answering your questions.

Here's a rule of thumb: in the early stages of the sales cycle, any statements that you make about yourself, your product, or your solution should be responses to the client's questions only. If they aren't, you're signaling that you are more interested in selling than in helping the client achieve his desired outcomes.

So, don't *tell, tell, tell.* Instead, engage in a dialogue and make sure all of your responses relate to the client's needs.

COMMUNICATION PREFERENCES AND MATCHING THE MEDIUM

In sales, as in life, the most important conversations should always take place face-to-face. That's because it's vitally important to convey that you care, and nothing proves it better than your physical presence. When the train comes off the track, your showing up says, "I am here to help because I care."

When it isn't possible to meet in person, these important conversations should take place on the telephone. E-mailing about a difficult situation tells the client that either you are afraid to have a conversation or the issue doesn't matter as much to you as it does to him.

Although the medium should match the importance of the message, ultimately you must use the method of communication your client prefers. For instance, I'm a phone guy, but I have a client—the CEO of a large company—who prefers text messaging. He is difficult to reach on the telephone but responds instantly to texts. When I asked him how he came to prefer text messaging, he replied that he hadn't thought about it. I then asked whether he had teenage children; he said he had two. Had his children taught him to text? He laughed and said they had, and that if he didn't text, he wouldn't be able to communicate with his kids at all. He soon began to prefer texting because the person communicating needs to get straight to the point.

Communication is more than just the message. You need to match the medium to the outcome of your message. We have to be careful about allowing the customer to determine the medium as a rule. Some clients' preferred method of communication won't serve the conversation. For example, they may prefer e-mail because they don't really want to discuss an uncomfortable issue when face-to-face communication would be more appropriate and improve the outcome. Carefully evaluate the message and medium needed to most effectively communicate.

THE THREE ELEMENTS OF EFFECTIVE COMMUNICATION

I had a great mentor in sales, a man who won more deals with fewer spoken words than I have ever witnessed. If there were an effectiveness metric that compared deal size to words spoken, he would surely be the most effective salesperson in the world.

He was a brilliant listener who asked questions, then sat quietly and listened to the clients' responses, prompting them with more questions only when they were completely finished speaking. He would let the client completely run out of words and then ask more questions to clarify. When he finally gathered all the information he needed, he would neatly summarize the points to make sure he had understood correctly. Only then would he explain how our service would meet their needs. He never "pitched" a client; he simply addressed their concerns. He spoke simply and he always told the truth, even when doing so was risky.

My mentor had the three attributes of effective communication. They are as follows:

- **Curiosity:** Great communicators are naturally curious, asking questions because they have a sincere desire to know. They are more interested in following the path to understanding than in pitching their own ideas.
- **Interest:** Effective communication is built on genuine interest in other people, and interest comes from caring. (You may want to go back and read chapter 3 again; it's that important.) The best salespeople make it easy for their clients to buy from them because they communicate that they are truly interested.
- **Candor:** Customers want an honest salesperson, someone they can trust. They need to hear the unvarnished truth about the challenges that lie ahead as well as the costs. Your customers deserve full disclosure; to withhold information is to be dishonest. Being transparent

about pluses, minuses, costs, and commitments (time, training, etc.) ensures that your clients will be comfortable with your solution and know you are putting their objectives ahead of your own.

HOW TO IMPROVE YOUR ABILITY TO COMMUNICATE

If you're brimming with curiosity, interest, and candor, you're probably already an effective communicator. You automatically transmit your concern and desire to help by listening with attention and interest, asking great questions, and refraining from rushing into your "pitch." The information and ideas you offer arise naturally as part of a dialogue between you and the client or prospect.

If you aren't a naturally effective communicator, a few ways to improve your communication skills follow. As you practice them and take them to heart, you'll likely find that you are becoming more curious about your clients and prospects, more interested in them, and more willing to do what it takes to solve their problems.

1. Practice Being an Exceptional Listener.

First, postpone your desire to speak. After you ask a question, listen to the answer with a strong desire to understand. Focus completely on your client and what she says, and don't plan what you will say in response. I have found that waiting silently for four beats after the client has finished often prompts her to speak some more. And what comes out then is often very important and revealing. A client may say something like, "We really just need to improve our throughput here . . . [beat, beat, beat, beat] . . . and I guess we probably have a leadership challenge with the manager in this department." Ah! This last bit of information is precious.

Second, before you respond, prompt your client for more information. Ask him to clarify and explain what he means so you can gain a deeper understanding. Do not simply repeat what you heard; parroting every statement is annoying. Instead, say things like, "Share with me a little more about your managers in that department, if you can."

Finally, learn to take concise notes so you can look your client in the eye while he speaks, yet collect all the necessary information with 100 percent accuracy. I try to write down the key words that will prompt me to speak to the major points. Usually three or four words is enough, and an exclamation point reminds me of something I want to respond to later. When you are called on to respond, summarize what you have heard before making any statements of your own. Your summary sends a message that what your client said was important and gives him the opportunity to redefine problems and objectives.

Making a record of the key points is vital. If you are not taking notes, you are not truly listening. You may be hearing the words and even paying attention, but you are also sending a strong message that none of it is important enough to record for future reference.

2. Put Yourself in Their Shoes.

When you imagine yourself in another person's position and try to see the situation from her point of view, you naturally become more curious and interested—two of the three attributes of great communication. You will genuinely want to learn about how she operates, where she is succeeding and failing, the challenges she faces, and more. By doing so, you'll automatically become a more effective communicator.

While you're putting yourself into other people's shoes, take note of the words they seem to favor, words that may have special meaning to them. Their language can help you understand their view of the world and provide you with an insight into what they believe is important and why. Their word choices are meaningful, so use them in your conversations, presentations, and proposals.

If the client says, "This is our most strategic challenge," you might say, "In order to help you with your most strategic challenge. . . ." If they say, "This terrible throughput is killing us," you might say, "I understand that the throughput challenge you have is killing your productivity."

By using their words to explain your ideas, you demonstrate that you understand their view and have entered their world, at least to some extent.

Ask yourself, "What is really being communicated here?" And "Have I captured this correctly?"

3. Master the Art of Asking Great Questions.

You will do more to impress and influence your dream client with a great set of questions than with any statements you can make. So how do you come up with great questions? Start by asking yourself the following:

- What do you need to know about your clients' businesses? About their industry? About their personal wants and needs? Make a list of the questions you would ask to find out.
- What do you need to know about their challenges? Are they unhappy with their current situation? If so, why? What might compel them to make a change?
- What has prevented them from obtaining the results they need? How are they dealing with those challenges now? Who else from their team might be able to help overcome these obstacles? You might ask the clients, "What's prevented you from being able to improve your results in the past?"

Great questions help you uncover your clients' decision-making criteria and the source of their dissatisfaction, information you need to position your solution ideally. More important, asking penetrating questions challenges your clients to analyze their problems—and how to solve them—which can spark their decision to move ahead with you.

4. Write, Rehearse, and Use Scripts.

Have you ever been in a critical conversation and said something so stupid that you couldn't believe the words had escaped your mouth? Have you ever wanted to snatch something back the instant you said it? Avoid this experience by planning what to say, and send your message in the most effective way possible.

I can already hear you grumbling that scripts kill your creativity and you need to be able to think on your feet. I suggest you do both: write, rehearse, and use scripts—*and* think on your feet. No matter how well prepared you are, you should expect to see at least one curveball during any client interaction. Remember that planning and improvisation are not mutually exclusive. Using scripts isn't the same as sounding as if you were reading a script.

Begin by planning dialogues for your most important client interactions. Write down the exact language for each question you need to ask and each statement you need to make, using your very best language. Powerful language makes for powerful communication. For example, here are some questions I've used in my work:

- "Can I share some ideas with you?"
- "Can I ask you to collaborate with me on the solution we are building?"
- "I feel like we've done enough work to move forward from here. Can we go ahead and get started with a contract or is there still something you need in order to be 100 percent confident moving forward?"
- "What's your vision for the right solution?"
- "Who else are we going to need on our team if we really want to make this work?"

Write scripts for the questions you need to ask during discovery sales calls and presentations and when handling the common problems that occur in your business. Come up with questions to ask in response to the most common objections you receive. And write out the examples you give to demonstrate your capability to overcome the obstacles behind those objections.

If you've been in sales for any length of time, you already use scripts, although you may not be aware of it. Don't you find yourself repeating many of the same words when you open a dialogue or present the benefits of a particular solution? This is a script, though you might never have written anything down.

I've been in sales for years, yet I go through this script-writing exercise for every important conversation to ensure that my communication is clear, with no stumbling or gaffes. Planning ahead in this way also helps eliminate undesirable language—anything that might sound judgmental, insensitive, or defensive. Take the time *before* you speak to think about all of your language choices and how those choices can make you a better communicator.

Choose Successful Communications

You've undoubtedly interacted with plenty of salespeople who refused to listen to you and only tried to sell to you. You've struggled to share your needs with those who couldn't possibly hear you because they were so busy trying to get their own messages across. It's a frustrating experience, and you probably couldn't wait to show these people the door.

And, yet, there have also been times when you've dealt with a salesperson who listened to what you said, asked great questions, and didn't rattle off one pitch after another. You felt like she cared, like she wanted what was best for you. The transaction was pleasant, even enjoyable, and you went away feeling that you were better off than before—that you had won.

I ask you: Which type of salesperson do *you* want to be?

FIRST MOVE—DO THIS NOW!

On your next sales call, practice pausing for a four count after your prospective client stops speaking. Wait long enough for the person with whom you are meeting to begin talking again, should they want to. You are likely going to be uncomfortable with the silence, but stay in the moment and wait. As you get more comfortable, pause for a count of five or six before you speak. By remaining silent, you are giving the person with whom you are speaking room to finish their thoughts. Don't just practice this one at the office either.

RECOMMENDED READING

Goulston, Mark. *Just Listen: Discover the Secret to Getting through to Absolutely Anyone.* New York: American Management Association, 2010.

Kahneman, Daniel. *Thinking, Fast and Slow.* New York: Farrar, Straus and Giroux, 2011.

Patterson, Kerry, Joseph Grenny, Ron McMillan, and Al Switzler. *Crucial Conversations: Tools for Talking When the Stakes Are High.* New York: McGraw-Hill, 2012.

Chapter 9

ACCOUNTABILITY: OWNING THE OUTCOMES YOU SELL

The ultimate definition of accountability is being able to go to sleep at night knowing you gave it your all in integrity and honesty. Nobody can take that away from you.

—Amanda Holmes, CEO of Chet Holmes International

FINISH THIS SENTENCE: "I SELL ___."

If you answered with anything other than "outcomes," you are wrong. If you answered with your product, service, or solution, your answer is so off the mark that it might destroy your ability to succeed in sales.

There is an old saying in sales and marketing that comes from Theodore Levitt: "People don't want to buy a quarter-inch drill. They want a quarter-inch hole." In other words, your customers are interested in buying an outcome—what you actually sell them is just a means of obtaining it. Think of it this way: if your customer could get the quarter-inch hole without the drill, he would happily do so.

In the old days, salespeople sold to their clients, took orders, and collected their pay. Whether the purchased item succeeded or failed was the client's problem; the salesperson had already moved on to the next opportunity. Today, success in sales requires much more of you, the salesperson, for you are a large part of the value proposition. Your client is buying not just the outcome but *your* ability to deliver it. This means that you have to own the outcome, not just the sale.

Owning outcomes means accepting responsibility for delivering holes instead of drills. You sold your clients some improvement in their performance. Now you must deliver that improved performance. Otherwise, you have failed your client. Your job doesn't end when you deliver the product, implement the program, or execute the service you sold. It continues as you ensure that the promised outcome is delivered. All actions necessary to achieve the results are employed, even long after the contract has been filed away.

Outcomes are not easily obtained in complex business-to-business sales. That's why you must work with your team and your client's team to ensure the outcome you have sold. You must continue to be present, standing in the trenches, shoulder to shoulder with your client. You must hang in there when things are most difficult, make your presence felt, and use all your skills to ensure delivery of the promised outcome.

When you deliver what you're truly selling—a successful outcome—you build a strong reputation as someone who fulfills his or her promises.

LIKE OLD FISH, PROBLEMS STINK

Have you ever had this experience? You accurately diagnose your clients' needs and understand how to help them. You work closely with them to devise the right solutions. And yet, somehow, it all falls apart. It wasn't your fault. But you are still responsible for the outcome.

I had this experience dozens of times in the staffing business. It seemed like the more work I did with a client to develop a solution to his biggest, most strategic problem, the more likely the whole thing was to run aground on day one of implementation. Perhaps the employees, despite being well prepared for the job, didn't show up. Or the sophisticated timekeeping system we installed crashed right before payroll was due. Yet these problems never ended the relationship—because I showed up with my team and resolved the problems.

I learned the hard way that there is almost always a steep learning curve. I even started joking with my prospective clients that we would get things right on the third or fourth try. Many of them would respond by saying, "We're lucky if we get anything right before the third or fourth time ourselves." My joke was a painful admission, but the clients recognized that I was aware of the potential for problems, and they believed that I held myself accountable.

You are not perfect, and you don't need to be—but you do need to be prepared for the major challenges involved in selling complex business outcomes. Your clients may be angry, unhappy, or upset about "your" failure; that's inevitable. It's how you respond when the bullets start flying that shapes your future relationships and determines whether or not you keep these clients.

The longer problems go unresolved, the more your clients' dissatisfaction grows—and, once again, this is the very same dissatisfaction that gave rise to your opportunity to work with them in the first place. If you don't tackle problems quickly and directly, you'll be replaced as surely as you replaced the salesperson before you.

If the trouble is with your team, if it is struggling to deliver what you sold, you must step up and provide help and leadership. And the sooner you realize that your team needs assistance, the easier it is to prevent a small challenge from growing into a results-killing monster.

No matter how problems arise, kill them early. Time is not your friend in this instance.

OWN OUTCOMES, NOT TRANSACTIONS

You must own the outcomes that you sell, but that doesn't mean you own all of the individual transactions that make up those outcomes. You must ensure that everyone involved understands his role in a given transaction— that he delivers what was agreed to in a timely manner and follows up with the client. Still, you can't get bogged down in taking care of every individual transaction yourself. If you do, you are not selling. If you're not selling, you are failing your team, company, future clients, and yourself.

For example, let's say your client calls you because an order is lost or missing and he needs help from your team in tracking it down. You decide that because you handled the sale, you personally must help him. You spend a couple of hours hunting down orders, and then you call him back to give a status report. Your goal is to prove that you care and are accountable. But this also steals time from your real responsibilities. What you really need to do is hand off the management of transactions to your team.

Instead of tracking down the missing orders yourself, call the responsible person on your team, inform her of the problem, and give her all the information she needs. Tell her that the client is expecting her to call, and ask her to give you a regular status update. If she reports that she took care of the issue, then you can follow up with your client to confirm that it was resolved satisfactorily. If the problem continues or resurfaces, let the client know which additional resources you will utilize to create a more permanent fix.

Insist on owning your outcomes, but not the actual transactions. You best serve your clients and your company by managing outcomes and leaving transactions to the people who were hired to handle them.

KEEP YOUR OWN SCORE

Here's another thing you are accountable for: ensuring that your clients know when things are going *right*. Report on your own successes. Doing so will serve you well when there are problems—and when it's time to renew your agreements.

Your clients will make sure you know about everything that is not quite right. You may get 98.9 percent of things right, but when you sit down together to review your results, they'll focus on the 1.1 percent that went wrong. The best way to deal with this 1.1 percent is to keep your own score. No one will ever hold you accountable for failed results if you've already held yourself to a higher standard. When you hold yourself to a higher standard than anyone else can imagine, you always soar above the mark that others have set for you.

When you meet with your clients, report on your progress and demonstrate a command of the facts related to your performance. Identify any outstanding issues and proactively develop a plan of action for each one, thus proving that you are keeping your own score. Your clients will be less likely to hold you accountable if they see that you are doing so yourself.

Don't neglect to take credit for what *is* working, though. If your scorecard shows that you are performing at 98.9 percent, take credit for the work involved—mostly your team's work—in delivering those results. Your income is directly proportional to your ability to produce the desired outcomes, and the greater those outcomes, the greater your earnings. That's why it is just as professional to take responsibility for what *is* working as it is to take responsibility for what is not.

HOW TO BE ACCOUNTABLE FOR RESULTS

Taking accountability for superior outcomes transforms you, in your client's eyes, from a mere salesperson to a value-creating, trusted adviser. By following four steps and owning your outcomes, you can become a strategic partner and a key part of your client's team.

1. Move from Products and Solutions to Outcomes.

Understand that you no longer sell products or solutions. You sell outcomes in the form of performance acceleration and improved business outcomes. It is not difficult to understand this shift; what is difficult is taking responsibility and acting accordingly.

Instead of confirming that your product was delivered on time and the solution is working as expected, verify that the client has achieved the result you promised and that the solution produced the desired result—greater profitability, lower cost, greater competitiveness, or other outcomes.

Look at the deals you are working on now. What are you really selling? What are your customers really buying? After you make the sale, how will their businesses be transformed? Exactly which business outcomes trigger the transformation? How do you ensure that this happens?

These questions are not easy to answer. Ensuring that the outcomes you sold are achieved is difficult and requires all of the elements we have studied up to this point.

2. Verify, Verify, Verify.

Is the outcome you sold being achieved? What are the results? Answer these questions by verifying that what you sold is working. Call and make sure that what you sold is working. Make site visits and check in on the people who are using what you've sold. Check back even when things are going well, just to make sure that nothing has changed.

Too much can go wrong in a short time. Early results may be good and then disappear. *You*, however, can't disappear.

Manage outcomes by confirming that results have been achieved. If the promised results are not achieved, then make sure that the necessary changes are implemented and executed.

Verify. Verify. Verify.

3. Take Responsibility for the Outcome.

Regardless of your company's organizational chart or how responsibilities are defined in the project-implementation plan, you are ultimately responsible for what you sold. If you don't believe me, ask your clients who *they* believe is responsible. Or, more to the point, ask them who they think is responsible when the train goes off the tracks.

When you take responsibility, you empower yourself to act instead of waiting to be acted upon. Taking responsibility makes you the de facto leader. It sends the message, "I care more about the client getting the right outcome than anything else."

Your success demands that you take responsibility for the outcomes you sell. If outcomes don't measure up, do what is necessary to make changes. You own this.

4. Get Help! Rally the Troops!

Look at the deals you are implementing. What are the problems, challenges, and obstacles that may prevent your clients from achieving the outcomes you sold?

You don't have to solve these problems by yourself or do the heavy lifting alone. There are people on your team and your client's team who can, and should, help you. Part of being resourceful is remembering that you have resources—namely, people.

Ask yourself these questions: Whom do you need to help you fix things? Who has expertise on the subject matter? Who has the necessary political capital? Who has the budget? Who has the authority to make the changes? Who from your clients' teams can help?

Then get moving on a solution. Don't let a little problem grow into something much worse.

You Sold It, You Own It

When you fail to quickly address your clients' problems, you send them two messages: you don't care enough to make sure they receive the promised value of what you sold them, and you don't know how (or don't have what it takes) to fix what is broken. Either message can damage your reputation, prompting people to speak poorly of you and causing you to lose clients.

As soon as you realize a problem has arisen, call and meet with your client to gain a full understanding of the situation. Next, call your team and your client's team together to find a quick way to make improvements. You may need to pull in additional resources, such as members of your management team or even outside help. You may need to make changes in what you sold. But you *must* lead the effort to produce an acceptable outcome. You sold the outcome and the assurance that it would be delivered. Now you need to own it.

By fixing the problem, you demonstrate how much you care about your clients, how capable you are of making good on your promises, and how determined you are to do so—all excellent reasons that your clients should stay with you.

One More Time

I ask you again: What do you sell? You sell outcomes. And you own them, too.

FIRST MOVE—DO THIS NOW!

Right now there is someone you left hanging. You sold them something, it was delivered, and you moved on. You never called to check and see how they were doing with what you sold them, and you have no idea whether or not they are producing the outcome you promised. Call or visit that client (or clients) and follow up to make sure they are achieving the outcomes they bought and paid for. If they're not, do whatever is necessary to make sure they get those results.

RECOMMENDED READING

Bossidy, Larry, Ram Charan, and Charles Burck. *Execution: The Discipline of Getting Things Done*. New York: Crown Business, 2002.

Miller, John G. *QBQ! The Question behind the Question: Practicing Personal Accountability in Business and in Life*. New York: Penguin Putnam, 2004.

Chapter 10

MASTERING THE MIND-SET ELEMENTS TO CREATE INFLUENCE

Manipulation is to influence what electricity is to water.

—Jeff Shore, author of *Be Bold and Win the Sale*

MY MOTHER RAISED FOUR KIDS BY HERSELF. FORTUNATELY, SHE had an excellent role model—her own mother raised five kids by herself. My mother was, is, and will always be the greatest influence in my life. She is the most congruent person I have ever met; she is exactly what she appears to be and does exactly what she says she will do. She may not be the image that comes to mind when you think of a salesperson, but, while working as a straight-commission recruiter on a small draw, she willed herself to dial the phone over and over again, day after day, to support her children. In time, her confidence grew enormously. Now her clients love her, and so do her employees. She is a great salesperson because she has influence.

None of it is tactical—it's character. The lessons she taught me have stuck (even if I occasionally needed a reminder). Both our lives would have been easier had I recognized this fact earlier in my life.

The stereotypical notion of a salesperson (or a person who makes a living influencing others) is a smooth-talking, backslapping, slickly smiling hustler with a shine on his shoes. But today, influence hinges much more on good, solid character. Think about the people who have had very positive impacts on your life. They are probably more like John Wooden, legendary coach of the UCLA Bruins basketball team, than like P. T. Barnum. They are most likely quiet, centered, and trustworthy. That is the kind of person you can become by adopting the principles in this book.

THE ELEMENTS OF INFLUENCE

The elements of sales success are firmly interconnected: one builds upon the next, and each strengthens all of the others. Taken together, they create a powerful ability to influence others.

Influence is the ability to persuade others to take an action, behave differently, or believe something. The influence I am referring to is not tactical; it arises from who you are at your core. It grows from being someone worth listening to and following.

This kind of influence is created from four basic elements:

- **Character:** People follow people with character. Character is the inner strength on which trust is built. It reflects a higher set of values, mission, purpose, and beliefs.
- **Congruence:** As a congruent person, you are who you appear to be. Everything you say and do is in perfect alignment with your character. There is no disconnect between how you represent yourself and who you actually are.
- **Confidence:** To have confidence is to have a high level of self-assurance. You have the ability to create value, and you know it. So do your clients and dream clients.
- **Likability:** Likability is fundamental to trust. People trust and buy from you because they like you. Some salespeople have a tremendous

ability to create value, but if they are not likable and easy to do business with, they cannot be influential.

I once had a client that put out a national request for a proposal. This almost certainly meant that I would lose the couple of million dollars' worth of business the client was currently doing with me. All of the major players were invited to bid.

I was the last person to present. I came alone, even though all my competitors had brought their teams. I had not committed to any requirements that were specified in the request for proposal—new requirements, not part of what my company was currently doing for the client.

There were eleven people from the client's company sitting around the boardroom table. They asked me why I wouldn't commit to all the requirements my competitors had agreed to.

I told them that their requirements were impossible to keep. Pulling out the data I had collected during the time I'd worked with them, I showed how they were performing now and how it would be impossible to do better, or even as well, if I committed to their requirements.

I made a professional presentation, had a serious command of the facts, and told the truth, even though eleven people were unhappy hearing it. I took a risk, knowing I was putting the deal in jeopardy. Still, I was confident in my ability to create value for the client. I also tried hard to be entertaining during my presentation to increase my likability.

When I finished, the client's attorney said, "This is the first honest person to sit in that chair." My willingness to lose the deal by telling the truth was a testament to my character. That changed the game.

I was what I appeared to be. I told the truth, even when it was unpopular—even when it was not what the client wanted to hear. I demonstrated confidence and likability. As a result, I was able to exert influence. Although the company did choose a national provider, I was the only supplier who was able to retain its business in my market.

INFLUENCE AND THE ELEMENTS OF SALES SUCCESS

Taken together, the first nine elements of sales success build influence, because they help you develop the self-discipline, optimism, caring, and other characteristics that influence requires. No tricks or tactics can replace them; there are no shortcuts. The mind-set elements are the foundation upon which a long track record of sales success is built. This is why they come before the skill-set elements.

Let's look at the link between the mind-set elements and influence:

Self-Discipline: Self-discipline is the foundation of all the attributes and skills you need to succeed in sales. People who are unable or unwilling to keep the commitments they make to themselves can't influence others. Influencing others begins by first keeping your commitments to yourself.

Optimism: Your optimism enables you to persuade others that a better future is not only possible, but certain. It enables the creation of a positive vision. You can't be a pessimist and influence others; no one follows someone who believes that success is impossible. People follow people who believe success is inevitable.

Caring: People are impressed when they know that you care about them. By the same token, they are *not* impressed and *not* influenced by people who clearly don't care about them. The more self-oriented you are, the less you care. On the other hand, the more caring you are, the greater your influence.

Competitiveness: Being a strong competitor creates influence by translating your burning desire to win into a demonstration of your ability to help others achieve a positive outcome. No one is influenced positively by someone who is apathetic about winning.

Resourcefulness: Being creative and imaginative, plus having a network of resources to solve problems and build solutions, makes you influential. And when you create positive outcomes and find a way where none previously existed, you become highly influential.

Initiative: You influence other people by taking the initiative and being proactive. Actions speak louder than words. Apathy, the opposite of initiative, destroys your ability to influence other people. No one is influenced by complacency.

Persistence: Your indomitable spirit—your determination and willingness to persevere—impresses others. Your persistence adds to your influence because people know you can be counted on to continue when all others have abandoned the effort.

Communication: Good communication skills help you convey that you care about others, that you are curious about and interested in them, and that you will speak to them openly and honestly. Truly understanding your clients—their world, views, ideas, and values—makes you more influential.

Accountability: You can only be influential when you care about your clients' businesses and take all actions necessary to ensure that they receive the outcomes they paid for—and more. Accountability is an act of caring, and caring creates trust, which is the foundation of influence.

HOW TO BE A PERSON OF INFLUENCE

There are only two steps required to be influential, and they are easy to understand. But they can take months, years, decades, or a lifetime to perfect—so the sooner you get started, the better.

1. Start with the Nine Mind-Set Elements of Sales Success.

It's true that the routine tips, tricks, gimmicks, and so-called secrets of influence may help you persuade—or bamboozle—some of the people some of the time. But there is no shortcut to developing the kind of influence you need to succeed in sales. To create this kind of influence, you need to be someone worth listening to and someone worth following.

This kind of influence, real influence, is all about who you are at your core. It's about your honesty and integrity, your caring and optimism, and more. It is about mastering the nine elements that make up the first half of this book.

2. Build a Record of Proven Results.

You enhance your influence and ability to persuade others when you create a record of success. A history of delivering the results proves you have the experience and skills necessary to help others meet their goals.

This does not mean that you need to seem perfect or can't fail. Sometimes speaking openly about your failures does more to persuade your clients than pretending you are perfect does. Just be sure that your discussion of failures comes with a look at the lessons you learned from them. This allows you to turn failures into the scars that demonstrate that you are battle tested and wiser for it.

Make a list of your personal accomplishments. Write down the things that you have done that have given you the necessary experience. Make a list of your failures and what they taught you. If you haven't taken time to codify these lessons and you do it now, you'll thank me later. It's a powerful exercise.

The nine mind-set attributes are not just techniques to be memorized and slipped into a sales presentation. They must *become* you in the sense that you internalize them and make them the basis for *all* of your thoughts and actions with *all* of your clients and prospects in *every* situation. Better still, make them part of your everyday being, so much a part of you that you don't even have to think about them anymore. They should flow from your deepest level, reaching other people naturally and effortlessly.

There is no path to success in sales without the ability to influence. There is no path to influence without the correct mind-set.

FIRST MOVE—DO THIS NOW!

Who is the person who has had the greatest influence on you? Who is the person you unequivocally trust and follow because of their character? Make a list of five traits that make them someone with real influence. Then determine which of these traits you need to develop and make a list of the actions you can take to model your influencer. What do they do that you should be doing?

RECOMMENDED READING

Carnegie, Dale. *How to Win Friends and Influence People.* New York: Simon and Schuster, 1936.

Cialdini, Robert B. *Influence: The Psychology of Persuasion.* New York: Harper Business, 2006.

Maxwell, John C., and Jim Dornan. *Becoming a Person of Influence: How to Positively Impact the Lives of Others.* Nashville, TN: T. Nelson, 1997.

Shore, Jeff. *Be Bold and Win the Sale: Get out of Your Comfort Zone and Boost Your Performance.* New York: McGraw-Hill, 2014.

Part 2

SKILL SETS: THE ABILITIES OF SALES SUCCESS

To succeed in sales, you need to know how to achieve particular outcomes. Achieving those outcomes requires a certain set of skills. Without any one of these skills, your sales results will be less than they might be.

This section begins with the fundamental skills salespeople have needed for centuries: closing, prospecting, and storytelling (which we now call presenting). These skills are timeless, and you need to exhibit a very high competency in each of them.

From the fundamentals, we move into more challenging outcomes and a higher level of skills. We'll look at diagnosing and negotiating, both of which are necessary, but especially in complex B2B sales.

The final three elements are new skills for salespeople. They build on the prior skills in this section, but they are of a much higher order. They aren't yet commonly taught, coached, trained, or developed—but they should be! We'll look first at business acumen, which provides you with the ability to create real value for your dream clients. Change management helps you build a case for change and find consensus within your prospective client accounts. And you need an understanding of leadership to develop the skills to lead your team—and your client's team—even though you may not have a title that identifies you as the formal leader.

The final chapter in this section discusses differentiation. When we are finished here, you will be a person who makes a difference for your dream clients. You will be someone worth buying from, and you will have skills you need to create opportunities, to win deals, and to deliver for your clients.

Chapter 11

CLOSING: ASKING FOR AND OBTAINING COMMITMENTS

Selling isn't something you do to someone. It's something you do for and with someone.*

—Anthony Iannarino

ALEC BALDWIN'S PERFORMANCE IN THE 1992 MOVIE *GLENGARRY Glen Ross* is unforgettable. His character, Blake, is a top-selling salesperson sent to improve the results of a group of underperforming real estate salesmen. Blake pounds home the sales wisdom of the era: A-B-C ("always be closing") and A-I-D-A ("attention, interest, decision, action"). In other words, push, push, and push some more: always be closing!

By the time the movie was released, however, things had already begun to change in the real world. In 1988, Neil Rackham's book *SPIN Selling* examined the link between closing behavior and sales. His conclusion was intriguing. While more closing behavior did lead to more sales, that was only true if both price and risk were relatively low. Rackham's

---

* Because so much of what you read about closing will actually hurt you, I had to use a quote from yours truly to start you off on the right foot.

research showed that for larger sales, the opposite was true: as price and risk increased, aggressive closing behaviors began to work *against* the salesperson. Unfortunately, many salespeople, sales trainers, and sales leaders interpreted this to mean that instead of "always be closing," they should "never be closing."

That's why you may have said (or heard people say) things like, "I don't want to come across as being too *salesy*" or "I don't feel comfortable asking for things. I want to come across as consultative."

Thinking this way makes you much too soft—you can find yourself afraid to say anything that might be at all uncomfortable for your clients or yourself. This most certainly decreases your effectiveness and lengthens the time you need to win deals, and you'll end up underperforming for your clients and your company.

Selling effectively is *all* about gaining commitments. It does not mean that you are selfish, manipulative, or unethical. You can still remain the consummate consultative sales professional while asking for any and all of the commitments you need.

While it's true that you can go too far too fast when asking for commitments (especially the commitment to buy), fear can keep you from going far enough fast enough. It's a balancing act. You can't follow Blake's advice and shove the sale down the client's throat, but you can't be so soft that you continually avoid asking for the commitments you need—and there are several of them. Ten, in fact.

THE TEN COMMITMENTS NEEDED TO CLOSE A SALE

Many people think of closing as obtaining the final commitment, the commitment to buy (or decide). Closing is actually more complex than that—it involves obtaining *all* of the commitments that are critical to creating and winning opportunities. Closing happens in stages: you enter a stage every time you ask a customer to make a decision to move forward, whether you're at the end, middle, or very beginning of the sales process.

Let's take a look at the ten commitments you must obtain in order to close a sale.

1. **The commitment of time.** You can't create opportunities unless your clients commit to giving you some of their time. You gain this commitment in prospecting, which is a critical activity for sales professionals. You must ask for and secure a prospect's commitment of time very early in the sales process. This can sometimes be the most difficult commitment to obtain, because prospects are busy, constrained by budgetary issues, and perhaps jaded by experiences with bad salespeople.

2. **The commitment to explore.** As you work through the discovery phase, your clients are making their own discoveries about themselves and about you. You need a commitment from them to explore the ways you might work together to make changes and improvements.

3. **The commitment to change.** If your prospective clients aren't committed to change, what you have are leads, not opportunities. Neither their needs, their budgetary constraints, nor the value you can create for them means a thing at this point. You must first secure a commitment to change.

4. **The commitment to collaborate.** You may have the best solution in the world, but until your dream clients add their ideas and the solution changes from "yours" to "ours," you aren't where you need to be. Your prospective clients have ideas about what they need and how they need it delivered. Ask them to collaborate with you in building solutions.

5. **The commitment to build consensus.** Winning a large, complex opportunity requires commitment from your contact within the dream client as well as from its executive team, individual stakeholders, and the groups they represent. Get a commitment to meet with all the people on the buying committee, as well as those who will be impacted by what you deliver.

6. **The commitment to invest.** Your dream clients must commit to investing the time, energy, and money necessary to produce the desired results. This is crucial. If they could produce the same results without making these investments, they would already be doing so.

7. **The commitment to review your proposed solution.** *All* the stakeholders involved in making the decision must review the solution you propose so that you can receive their input and have an opportunity to make adjustments. Ask for this commitment to review once you are certain that your solution matches your prospective client's needs and will produce the desired outcome.

8. **The commitment to resolve concerns.** You need a commitment from your prospective client to give feedback on your presentation so that you can resolve any anxieties she may have. Such concerns may be resolved by providing proof, walking the client through an implementation plan, or simply by spending time answering her questions. Never leave a presentation without asking for a commitment to meet again to discuss any concerns.

9. **The commitment to decide (to buy).** You need to ask for a commitment to move forward together. This particular commitment is what we refer to as "the close." Without it, you get nowhere. However, this commitment is often mistakenly believed to be the only commitment that matters. In fact, earlier commitments are just as crucial but often are even harder to gain.

10. **The commitment to execute.** At this point, you've made the sale, and now you must help your dream clients execute and ensure that they get the outcomes you've sold them. This means that you must ask them to make the necessary changes that enable you to execute. Their commitment to execute is every bit as important as yours.

TO OBTAIN COMMITMENTS, CREATE VALUE

To get commitments from your prospects, you must earn the right to ask for them. If you have created value for your dream client and can explain the further value of moving forward together, then you have a right and a duty to ask for the commitment. But you must do the necessary work before asking.

At several points along the way, examine your interactions through your client's eyes. Seek to demonstrate your understanding of his situation as well as your ability to create value continually. Examples follow:

- When prospective clients are just beginning to recognize a need for change, create value by helping them explore and understand the current problem as well as the need for change. (Commitments 1, 2, and 3)
- Once they understand the need for change, help them decide what they require to move forward to a better future state. (Commitments 2, 3, and 4)
- When they evaluate their options, help them understand and select from the range of available choices. Clearly differentiate your offering from your competitors'. (Commitments 5, 6, 7, and 8)
- When they are trying to make an informed decision, help resolve their concerns and mitigate risk. (Commitments 5, 6, 7, and 8)

You'll gain commitments more easily when you link the value you create during one sales interaction to the value you will create in the next interaction. To create value on *every* sales call, at every step along the way, you must leave the prospect or client in a better position than she was in before the call. This "value chain" makes it easier for your dream clients to say yes at every step along the way. When you know you have created value during every single sales interaction, you can naturally and comfortably ask for her business.

To obtain a commitment, you'll need to be able to explain the value of moving forward. This is easy at the end of the sales cycle. When you have a return on investment (ROI) analysis in hand, it is easy to explain the value of moving forward. But what about at the beginning of the sales cycle and at all of the little steps between opening and closing?

Every sales call must have its own value proposition. If you ask for a first meeting, you have to promise some insight that your dream client can use—whether or not he ever hires you. If you ask your dream client to give you time to meet the additional stakeholders, you have to promise that you will help build consensus within that group, making his job easier.

During the discovery phase of the sales cycle, give your dream client a fresh perspective on his situation, a deeper understanding of the implications of not changing, and a clear vision of how his future will be made better. Those are value-creating outcomes.

Maybe you need to acquire additional information from other stakeholders and decision influencers within your client's company. How do clients benefit from granting you access to the additional stakeholders? They benefit because you gain a greater understanding of their needs, and you develop the relationships that will later allow you to provide the best solution. When you ask for the commitment to grant access to influencers, this is the pitch you need to make. It tells the clients the value you intend to create.

VALUE, VALUE, VALUE

No matter how large or small the sale, you have to ask for and obtain the commitment to do business. In fact, you will be asking for many commitments during the long sales process. Each and every commitment is a closing; all are opportunities to create value for your clients, and creating value leads to sales and satisfied customers.

THREE WAYS TO IMPROVE YOUR ABILITY TO CLOSE

All the commitments in this chapter are important. However, this is a chapter on closing, so we have to deal with asking your prospect for the business, and we have to get it right.

You are right to resist hard-sell closing techniques. If a close has the name of a great figure from history—as in "the Ben Franklin close"—or some other clever title, it is no longer useful, especially for salespeople in a B2B setting. If it's in a "Dummies" book, it isn't going to help you. In fact, it most likely will create resistance.

The hard-sell closing techniques of the past may be dead, but the need to ask for commitments from the client is not. Here are some powerful tools to help you ask for commitments that lead to the close without violating your client's trust.

1. Know Your Outcome.

Do you truly know which specific outcome you seek? People often mistake activity for outcomes, but they are not the same thing. A sales call is an activity, not an outcome. The desired outcome of a sales call is a commitment that moves an opportunity forward.

Before every sales call, decide what you want the outcome to be, and remember that it must always be a commitment that moves the sale forward. This is often the most important, yet most overlooked, piece of planning for sales calls.

I can't tell you how many times I have heard a salesperson say something like, "They loved us! They loved what we do, and they are so aligned with our values. It was a great meeting." When I ask about the commitment they gained, I hear, "They said they'd call us sometime soon." No commitment was asked for and none was gained. The salesperson has failed, and she has failed her dream client by putting off the date when a commitment can be made.

Draw up a list of the stages of your sales cycle with all of the commitments you need to move a deal from beginning to final closing event. Refer to this list before every sales interaction so you know which commitment you intend to obtain.

2. Use Natural, Honest Language.

The best closing language is other-oriented, not self-oriented. Instead of tricks or manipulation, use honest, natural language and simply ask for the client's business. Be polite, professional, and direct. You might say something like this:

> Thanks for allowing me to present our solution today. What we've put together will help you achieve the desired outcomes that you shared with me during this process. I want you to know that we will own—and deliver—our part of those outcomes. If we have done enough to earn your business, I would like to ask you for the opportunity to help with this project. Can we begin working on this project now?

Don't worry if potential clients respond by reciting their objections and concerns. That can be a good thing, for now you can work on resolving them. If they don't have any objections, yet you still do not get the commitment to sign an agreement, you might ask, "Is there something else we need to do first?" But no matter how they respond to your presentation, never leave a meeting without saying something like, "We really want the opportunity to work with you, and we won't let you down."

By asking for your clients' business directly, you demonstrate that you truly want to work with them and are likely to be just as direct in helping them achieve their goals. You demonstrate that you are a strong competitor.

The previous example of closing language assumes a complex sale. In a transactional sale, where both price and risk are low, you can ask for the clients' business much earlier in the process and more directly because there is less value created. You might say something like this:

> We know enough to start helping you in this area. Is there an order I can start working on for you now?

This is simple, direct, and professional. It builds your client's trust and demonstrates your professionalism.

3. Ask for Commitments *after* Creating Value.

Closing is natural and easy as long as you have earned the right to ask for and receive it—which you do by creating value during each and every sales interaction.

Make a list of the benefits the client will receive by agreeing to move forward in the sale. If you're not sure what to write down, ask yourself the following questions:

- How does the client benefit from agreeing to move forward to the next stage of the sales cycle with me? What does she get out of it?
- If at some point the client goes no further in the process, will she still have received good value for the time she invested?
- What can I do to make sure this meeting is worth the client's time?

Answering these questions can help you ask for the commitment, confident that your dream client will say yes.

Closing is the first skill or attribute you must possess. Not because you need to close a deal but because you need to obtain the commitment to open the possibility of working together. This is the first and most critical commitment you must obtain. All other closes follow it.

FIRST MOVE—DO THIS NOW!

I really want you to take action on the ideas in this chapter now. Look at the active opportunities in your sales pipeline. Identify the deals where you have no scheduled next action that your prospective client has committed to take. Write down the commitment you need from each

---

one next to their name (or enter it in your customer relationship management [CRM] system). Pick up the phone and call the biggest, most important opportunity on your list and ask them for the commitment you should have asked them for at the end of your last meeting with them.

RECOMMENDED READING

I don't have any books to recommend here. Most everything that has been written is out of date and offers tactics that will actually make you less effective and cost you deals.

Chapter 12

PROSPECTING: OPENING RELATIONSHIPS AND CREATING OPPORTUNITIES

Prospecting is the lifeblood of your organization. Done well, it will provide abundance. Done poorly, and you will fail. No mystery here.

—Miles Austin, www.fillthefunnel.com

YOU PROBABLY ALWAYS THOUGHT THAT PROSPECTING CAME BE-fore closing, but to create an opportunity, you must be able to ask for and gain the first two commitments you need to move a lead into true prospect status: the commitment of your prospect's time and the commitment to explore working together. Unfortunately, both are becoming more and more difficult to get.

The business environment has changed radically over the past two decades, thanks to globalization, the Internet, and some major recessions. As a result, we have had to make drastic alterations in the way we sell.

Globalization has forced us to become competitors in the world marketplace. You can no longer be "the only game in town" when the "town" is the whole world. With so many more salespeople and sales organizations going after the same clients, it has become harder and harder for any one competitor to stand out in the crowd. If this isn't true for you yet, just wait. It will be.

The Internet has shifted the balance of power. Whereas sellers used to control information, the Internet has given buyers access to more information and more choices than ever. And it is easier for buyers to find someone who looks a lot like you to sell them what they need if they don't believe you are treating them fairly.

Making matters worse, the United States has just suffered through a decade that began and ended with major recessions. During these downturns, companies focused on cost cutting as a means to survive—a practice that continues unabated. Purchasing departments and chief financial officers have gained power, and salespeople now face buyers who are more concerned about price than they previously were. This is true even when the buyer isn't the person charged with evaluating the financial aspects of a deal. Today, "tech" folks and people on the operations team are also concerned about price. I call this new buyer psychology "post-recessionary stress disorder." It causes everyone to focus on price rather than cost.

The upshot of all these changes is that it can be significantly more difficult to get your dream clients' attention, let alone a commitment for their time. It's harder to create opportunities—yet without opportunities, you can't produce results.

OPENING IS THE NEW CLOSING

The contacts in your dream clients' companies are busier than ever. They have been downsized, rightsized, and reorganized countless times and simply have no margin of error—or time—to spare. They are also under incredible pressure to produce financial results. Even your contacts with little formal authority are responsible for a line on a profit-and-loss statement.

The contact you need inside your dream client doesn't have time to meet with salespeople, especially those who can't help her produce better results *right now*. She doesn't have time for professional visitors and time wasters. She refuses your request to meet because she refuses every salesperson's request to meet. Since she can't tell who is truly a value creator, she says no to everyone.

This dearth of opportunities can make you more likely to pursue unqualified opportunities; after all, to a starving person, everything looks like a meal. But this will only steal your time without moving you any closer to your goals.

In our current market, having a solid prospecting plan is critical. If you have no plan and no targets, your efforts will be inconsistent and ineffective. You will become worried and start to chase after unqualified opportunities—wasting time, exhausting yourself, and practically guaranteeing failure. That's why it's crucial that you sit down and construct a thoughtful, deliberate prospecting plan that delivers results *right now*.

MAKE A PROSPECTING PLAN

Prospecting must be done deliberately and consistently, with a definite goal in mind at all times. Here's a five-point plan that will help you succeed:

1. Identify Your Targets.

Make a list of your dream clients, including all the contacts in each organization who would be affected by a decision to switch to a new partner (namely, you). Think this through very carefully; you cannot succeed if you have chosen the wrong targets. Do the companies on your list have the kinds of problems and challenges that you can solve? Will your value proposition be so compelling that they will quickly perceive that value and be willing to pay for it?

For most salespeople, a list of sixty dream clients is a good start—you can contact fifteen per week and still have time for other prospecting work. At this rate, each month, you can communicate something of value to all sixty of them.

Incorporate every means of identifying targets that is applicable to your industry. These may include the following:

- **Client referrals:** Nothing is more powerful or effective than referrals from existing clients and customers. Ask your current clients or customers to refer you to someone else for whom you can create similar value. Some salespeople are resistant to asking their clients for referrals. I've found that they are the same ones who fear and resist cold calling. Something to ponder, no? But both are absolutely necessary in sales. To succeed in sales, you have to pick up the phone and ask for referrals, just as you need to make cold calls.

- **Vendor referrals:** The vendors who sell products and services to your company have their own sales relationships. Ask them to make introductions for you, and you can offer to do the same for them. Swapping introductions works well when you share some of the same targets as your vendors.

- **Cold calling:** Picking up the phone and making cold calls is an extremely effective way to generate new business, second only to referrals. That's why it must be one of the primary tools in your arsenal. If your plan doesn't include telephone work, you will not produce the results you are capable of. If you need help with cold calling, download my e-book *How to Crush It, Kill It, and Master Cold Calling Now*, at http://www.thesalesblog.com/resources.

- **Networking events:** Networking events give you an opportunity to meet your dream clients face-to-face. Find local business networking events that your target clients are likely to attend. Put these events on your calendar and go.

- **Conferences and trade shows:** Conferences and trade shows are great opportunities to be in the same places as your dream clients. Of course, you have to justify your trip to a conference or trade show by generating real sales opportunities. Fortunately, your dream clients must also justify their trips by meeting people who can help—that is, by meeting you. For once, they may be as eager to meet you as you are to meet them. Take advantage of the opportunity. Get the attendee list ahead of time and schedule meetings.

- **Social media:** If you love social media, you are probably relying on it too heavily as a generator of inbound leads. If you hate social media, you are probably ignoring one of the most effective tools available. It must be part of your plan but should not be your whole plan. Use LinkedIn, Twitter, Facebook, and any other social sites that make sense to share ideas that show you are a value creator. Promoting your ideas will make it easier to open relationships.
- **E-mail:** E-mail still works—if your e-mail has a great subject line with as few words as possible, and the body of the e-mail offers something of value with no "ask." It should, however, also include a very brief note saying that you are going to call to make the ask. E-mail is very low on the prospecting list because it's no longer as effective as it once was, at least for B2B sales organizations. Too many salespeople hide behind e-mail, and most of it is simply filtered out.
- **Mail:** There is nothing like a handwritten note. Good old-fashioned notes and letters still work. Consider them to really help nurture relationships.

2. Focus on Nurturing Your Dream Clients.

In sales, nurturing can be defined as "creating value before you claim any." You make deposits into the relationship by creating value, often by sharing ideas that can make a positive difference for your dream clients whether or not they hire you. Many sales organizations believe they should withhold their best ideas, but without a willingness to share, you cannot show that you are a value creator with the ability to make a difference.

Make a list of the ideas and tools at your disposal that prove you are a value creator. For example, perhaps your company has produced a white paper that has ideas relevant to your dream client. Send it, along with a handwritten note identifying the most salient parts. Do you have research about your industry, or your dream client's industry, that can help make positive changes in the ways they do business or spur them to make new, constructive decisions? Does your experience allow you to offer some unique insights worth sharing?

Start by identifying twelve tools you can use to create value and decide how you will use these to nurture your dream clients. Then, on your calendar, make a note of when you are going to use each tool to create value. You'll soon shift from being an unknown to being a known value creator.

3. Build Campaigns.

Prospecting is a campaign, not an event. It's a series of "touches" that lead to a conversation and an opportunity to meet and figure out how and where you can make a difference.

Your first "touch" might be a connection request on LinkedIn, followed by a personal e-mail that includes some value-creating content—without the "ask." You might follow that up with a copy of a white paper or case study that shares a big idea, again with no "ask." Then you might make a call to request a short meeting. I find that twenty to thirty minutes is a low-level commitment that a majority of people will easily agree to, mostly because they can bail out if the salesperson appears to be wasting their time.

Then you can begin to build. Shoot for eight connections with prospects over the course of thirteen weeks. The number eight shows your commitment to connect and that you are going to persist. It also says that you are about improvement and results. Too often, salespeople communicate once and then go away. Or they try calling to schedule an appointment every single day. The trick in building a campaign is to provide value with every touch. Directly ask for an appointment in only two of those touches. The other six touches are gifts of value for your prospects, given without an "ask." Remember, we are creating value so that we can earn the right to capture value later. It's a campaign, not an event.

4. Use Planned Dialogues.

Your initial conversations with prospects are crucial because you only get one opportunity to make a first impression. Make sure it's a great impression by building that dialogue in advance, ensuring that you are using the most effective language possible.

Write out your prospecting conversations *before* you call or meet, and practice them out loud. Practice responding to brush-offs and objections as well.

Practice until you're perfect and then ease up. Don't reel off one memorized paragraph after another. You want a script, but you don't want to sound scripted.

5. Make Prospecting a Daily Discipline.

If you had sixty dream clients, it might take you a full day to send each one of them a value-creating e-mail. That's impractical, and you would get nothing else done.

You can, however, send a personal value-creating e-mail to fifteen dream clients a week, rotating all sixty through the cycle once a month. You can also follow up each of those fifteen e-mails with a personal phone call the following week. That would equal three personal, value-creating e-mails and three personal phone calls a day—which you could easily do in an hour.

PUT YOUR PROSPECTING PLAN INTO ACTION

Even the best prospecting plan is useless if you don't put it to work. Here's how to make it a priority:

- **Put prospecting first.** You can't cram prospecting. It must be a daily discipline. Block out time every day for this activity.
- **Be consistent in your efforts.** You don't control when your dream client might become dissatisfied enough with his current situation to make a change. You might call every week for years, only to have your meeting requests refused every time. But as soon as the prospect becomes even slightly unhappy, your request will suddenly be granted. You can't predict when that might happen, so you can never go away. Keep calling your dream clients, no matter what.
- **Vary your approach.** Most salespeople prospect using the one method that feels most comfortable to them. But that's not necessarily the method of communication your prospective clients prefer. *They* pick the channel that they respond to, so you need to use all of them. This includes the telephone, even if you are young and hate cold calling. This also includes LinkedIn and other social media, even if you have a few gray hairs and aren't all that interested in these new tools for communication. Use all of the tools at your disposal until you find what's best for each prospect.
- **Separate research from prospecting.** Research is one type of work and prospecting is another; blending the two slows your prospecting. Speed your progress by doing research separately from prospecting. Take the time to build your list of dream clients and all of the potential contacts you need within those companies. Then, and only then, should you do your prospecting. If you need to do more research, invest the time required, and then get back to the work of connecting.
- **Eliminate distractions.** When it's time for you to do your prospecting, turn off your e-mail, the Internet, and your smartphone. Focus. Tell your peers that you have a newfound discipline and you need their support; you'll catch up with them later. Hang a sign on your door that says, **DO NOT DISTURB! PROSPECTING!** If you do not have a door, use string to hang this sign over your desk. The more focused you are on prospecting, the greater your results will be, and the faster they will occur.

- **Make the plan your own.** Don't gauge the amount of effort you need to put into prospecting by looking at what other salespeople do. I know a salesperson who easily books 40 percent of the contacts she connects with. Yet if someone else made as few calls as she did, he would probably fail because her combination of approach/product/price and other factors is not the same as his. You have to invest the time necessary for *you*. Do what you need to do and stick to your plan. Never mind what somebody else is doing.
- **Focus on the outcome.** Through all the ups and downs of prospecting, always keep your eye on the prize: a meeting. Know that you'll get those meetings if you persevere.

DON'T WAIT UNTIL YOU NEED IT

Your first challenge in sales is creating sufficient opportunities. And this depends almost entirely on how you invest your time and energy, the decisions you make, and how well you plan and execute your prospecting.

There's always something you can do that seems more important than prospecting. The work that shows up on your desk or streams in via your telephone and e-mail in-box always feels more urgent. That's because prospecting never really appears urgent—until it is. Unfortunately, once you urgently need to prospect, it's already too late to do anything about it. Prospecting requires a lot of discipline, no doubt about it. But, as I said back in chapter 1, self-discipline is the cornerstone of success—in sales and in life.

You must do enough prospecting to create the opportunities you need to make your quota. You also need to prospect enough to build a pipeline that allows you to lose opportunities and still make your number based on your close rate. Prospecting is the discipline of sales champions.

FIRST MOVE—DO THIS NOW!

Pick up the phone and call your top three dream clients. That's it. Win or lose, prospecting requires that you take action, and this is the fastest, most reliable way to schedule an appointment with a prospect. What? It's nighttime and you're not at work? Then call first thing tomorrow morning. Don't cheat yourself here. Do the work!

RECOMMENDED READING

Blount, Jeb. *Fanatical Prospecting: The Ultimate Guide to Opening Conversations and Filling the Pipeline by Leveraging Social Selling, Telephone, E-Mail, Text, and Cold Calling.* Hoboken, NJ: Wiley, 2015.

Konrath, Jill. *SNAP Selling: Speed up Sales and Win More Business with Today's Frazzled Customers.* New York: Portfolio, 2010.

Weinberg, Mike. *New Sales. Simplified. The Essential Handbook for Prospecting and New Business Development.* New York: American Management Association, 2013.

Chapter 13

STORYTELLING: CREATING AND SHARING A VISION

Stories push us past numbers and into our feelings. Used for business, a good story beats a spreadsheet any day.

—Chris Brogan, **author of** *Trust Agents*

I BEGAN CHAPTER 9 BY ASKING YOU TO COMPLETE THIS SEN-
tence: "I sell _____." Then I pointed out that the correct answer is always "outcomes." All salespeople sell outcomes and *only* outcomes, though they may be produced by machines, pencils, billing software, temporary employees, ice cream, or whatever the seller actually delivers to the client.

You sell outcomes—correct. But how do you sell outcomes? You sell outcomes by telling a story that envisions a better future for the customer.

Storytelling is the last of the three foundational sales skills, the first two being closing (gaining commitments) and prospecting (creating opportunities). Although I present storytelling last, that doesn't mean it should be relegated to the end of the process. Far from it—you should start telling stories from moment one.

WHAT A STORY IS AND ISN'T

A story is a vision of what could be and storytelling is the process of sharing that vision. It isn't just an amusing or dramatic tale—or a slide deck that bores your dream client to tears with the story of your company's founding and the logos of all of the great companies you work with. Storytelling isn't just a presentation with smooth gestures, clever turns of phrase, and great graphics.

A story is a narrative that conveys a message or meaning. Your words, images, and perhaps even numbers transport your listener from one place and time to another. Your story presents a vision of how your prospective client can move from the status quo to a better future.

It doesn't matter whether you tell a prepared story or you speak off the cuff; whether you use a PowerPoint presentation, sketch something on a napkin, or have no illustrations at all. You must take your prospects on a journey and move them emotionally. Effective stories always stir the emotions.

WHAT MAKES A GREAT STORY?

Stories have been told since the beginning of time. One of the greatest is Homer's *Odyssey*, an epic tale of struggle, danger, adventure, and love, culminating in a long-sought outcome. The hero returns home, slays the villains, rescues his wife, and is reunited with his son. Like all great stories, the *Odyssey* has vision, values, and an outcome. It also features a hero who faces challenges and is assisted by others along the way.

Any story you tell a prospective client must have a hero (your client), and that hero must be ably assisted (by you). Together, you and your client will slay the dragons (solve problems) that arise along the way as you journey to the desired outcome. The story must also represent your values, the underlying reasons why you do what you do the way you do it. Its outcome must be a vision of the client's future, showing how wonderful things will be if he will only allow you to assist him on the journey. In short, the ingredients of a great story are the following:

- A hero
- An assistant
- Challenges
- A "dragon"
- A vision
- Values
- A wonderful outcome

In the story you tell your prospective client, the hero is in a predicament: sales are down, software wasn't designed to handle the flow of information they're facing, staff is depleted, costs have skyrocketed—any number of problems have arisen. The hero may have tried to move forward on his own or with the help of others, but he has always been beaten back. Now you arrive on the scene, unsheathe your sword (the solution), and aid the hero in moving forward.

Naturally, at some point, a dragon appears. (Stories are boring without terrible dragons threatening to destroy everything in sight, including our hero.) The dragon may take the form of an unexpected glitch in the software package you sold to the hero, an economic crisis, or a competitor who steals your client's market share and puts pressure on the margins. Always loyal, you stand shoulder to shoulder with the hero as you analyze the dragon and prepare a plan of action. Ever resourceful, you offer an excellent solution. And if that doesn't work, you come up with another and another until the dragon has finally been slain.

The hero can now march triumphantly to a better place. The crisis has vanished, and the hero is set to enjoy a happier and more profitable future.

This is the paradigm for the "heroic journey," one of the most powerful and enduring story forms ever devised. The same formula was used in the *Star Wars* movies. Thus, you can think of your client as Luke Sky-walker and yourself as the wise Yoda. (Hat tip to Nancy Duarte of Duarte Design for the shift in perspective from thinking that we, the salespeople, are Skywalker!)

CRAFTING YOUR STORY

Although using a story like this may feel like you're telling your client a fairy tale, you're not. You're simply using a powerful form to make diffi-cult issues easier to understand, more visual, and more emotionally ac-cessible.

Most likely, your story will take the form of a *case history*—a story about another client or company you've worked with—or a *visioning story*, which paints a picture of your client's future without reference to any others.

Here are a few things to think about when putting your story to-gether:

- **Begin in the future.** It's very tempting to begin by rehashing the prob-lems the client already knows she faces, or with facts about your company history. But these are stale, boring, and amazingly unmoti-vating approaches. Instead, start your story by painting a picture of the outcome—your client's fantastic future and the wonderful results you will help your client attain. Be sure to put her in the starring role.

  Here's how it might sound: "Sales are way up. New clients are being acquired. And your wallet share is growing." Or "Production throughput is now at 105 percent, overtime hours are no longer nec-essary, and bonuses have been restored."

- **Describe how you will get there together.** Explain to your dream cli-ent what it will take to produce the necessary results and talk realis-tically about the work that needs to be done. As you detail how you will produce these results together, you have the opportunity to dif-ferentiate yourself from your competitors. You can also explain why you make certain choices and why you deliver your services in a certain way. This gives your dream client a clear idea of the value you will create.

Here's how it might sound: "The sales force has been retrained. They have been given a new mind-set, a new skill set, and the process and playbook they need to produce results." Or "The old equipment has been replaced, so the downtime that caused production issues and overtime has been eliminated. Productivity is now at bonus levels."

- **Describe the challenges you will face together.** Challenges are the dragons you must slay together. Despite what you might think, horrible fire-breathing dragons are good. After all, if it were easy to produce the results your client needs, someone else would have done it already. By facing challenges head-on, you can become a trusted adviser. So speak about the dragons openly and honestly, describe how you have overcome similar challenges in the past, and show how you will do so again. Pretending to your client that there will be no challenges will set off warning bells signaling that you are not to be trusted.

  Here's how you might describe the challenges: "To produce these results, we are all going to have to commit to change, even when it feels uncomfortable. And we will have to hold everyone accountable. This won't be easy. But we are certain that, together, we can do this." Or "The challenges we face are financing the machinery and keeping productivity up to the existing levels while we make these changes."

- **Touch on emotions.** Keeping it subtle, use language and ideas that touch the emotions. One way to do this is to talk about how other people have felt when faced with the same situation.

  Here's how it might sound: "The sales managers we worked with were stressed out, and they were worried about missing their numbers for the last four quarters. But once we worked together to develop a plan they believed in, they felt a tremendous sense of relief." Or "The employees felt unappreciated. They were working too many hours and calling in sick to try to get some time back with their families. This impacted both the business and their sense of community."

- **Work in your values.** It can sometimes be difficult to talk about your values in an authentic and persuasive manner. In fact, when you flat-out tell people things like, "We are honest and trustworthy," you usually sound phony. Instead, use your story to subtly demonstrate your values. Don't explicitly state your values; let them come through on their own.

  Here's how it might sound: "Throughout this entire process, we are going to provide your team with full access to every decision we make." Or "You might feel that some of these meetings are redundant, but we've found that including your team members and keeping them informed keeps them engaged in the process. They also won't need to worry about changes being made without considering the impact they'll have down the line."

As you craft your story, remember that your clients are sophisticated people who are able to see through exaggerations and sniff out flattery. Don't risk breaking their trust by turning your story into a tall tale. Stick with the truth! Honesty is one of the core values common to successful salespeople.

YOUR STORY LIVES BEYOND THE TELLING

The sales process continues long after you leave the building, which means that the stories you tell your prospective clients will probably be shared with others.

Once you leave a meeting, the contacts who support you will step in as your surrogates, sharing your stories with their peers. They will be asked about you, your ideas, and your ability to make a difference. Stakeholders in your client's company, including the executive management team, will ask your contacts tough questions about why they should make a change, why they should choose you, and why it's necessary to do anything right now.

By providing your contacts with the stories and information they need to back you up, you prepare them to share your vision and values with their teams. Your contacts may not remember anything from your slide deck, but they *will* remember your stories.

HOW TO BECOME A BETTER STORYTELLER

Before you can become a good storyteller, you must collect some good stories to tell. You don't need to dream up every story from scratch. Look to your own life, especially your sales life. You probably have all kinds of stories, many of which illustrate lessons that can help your clients succeed. Start by thinking about your experiences in sales and serving your customers, and then answer the following questions:

- Which stories are most compelling?
- Which illustrate the lessons that you have learned?
- Which help create a vision of what is possible?
- Which show that you were instrumental in helping your clients slay their dragons?

Your company also has a collection of great stories about how it helped its customers face their challenges. Your peers also have stories. It doesn't matter if a story isn't yours; if it illustrates the vision you want to share, it is worth telling.

Once you've collected your stories, do some work to improve your ability to tell them well. Here are some ideas to get you started.

1. Find the Arc.

Every great story has an arc, a progression of events that takes the main character on a journey that rises to a climax and then settles into a conclusion. There is always a certain amount of conflict; there are obstacles to be overcome. The conflict is what creates drama and makes a story compelling, as we witness the character's struggles to get somewhere, do something, or reunite with someone. The classic love story goes from "boy meets girl" to "boy loses girl" to "boy wins girl back" to "boy marries girl." The loss of the girl (the conflict) is what begins the journey—the boy must now work to get her back. This is the beginning of the story arc.

Look for the arc in your own stories. Identify the conflict, the elements that produce drama—the problems, challenges, and obstacles you needed to overcome together. Your story arc might take you from "client needed results" to "client tried this and failed" to "client worked with us in a way neither of us ever imagined" to "client got great results."

As you analyze your stories, ask yourself the following questions:

- What were the challenges you and your client faced together?
- What were the unexpected obstacles?
- What surprising ideas helped you to succeed?
- What lessons did you learn?

I once worked with a client who was having trouble acquiring the people they needed for peak season. Their competitors were all located in the very same area, and to corner the market on peak season help, their neighbors had raised their pay rates high enough that my client's pay rate was no longer attractive to the people they needed (our challenge). We had long suggested that our client pay more to ensure they met their peak season needs, though they refused the idea. Now we were stuck, and neither we nor our clients were certain how we were going to find the people we needed (the obstacles).

We called a meeting and provided our client with a salary survey and some other metrics and suggested they share this information with their clients so that we could ask them to help with the pay increase we needed to ensure their success (a surprising idea). They hadn't thought of asking their clients for help, and they were a little afraid to do so. Still, they took a chance. Not all of their clients agreed to the increase, but enough said yes and we were able to increase the rate to a rate even greater than their competitors'. By providing them with ammunition to take to their clients, we worked together and found success (lesson learned).

Once you've found your arc, build your story around it. For more about arc and becoming a master storyteller, see Robert McKee's book *Story: Substance, Structure, Style, and the Principles of Screenwriting.*

2. Find the Details That Bring Your Story to Life.

Details give life to a story, so make sure your stories have some—though not too many—and avoid those given simply for the sake of detail. Just add enough details to make your story real and alive. Consider including details such as the following:

- How the client found you
- The characters involved
- What they were trying to do and why
- What it meant to them
- Why the client's stakeholders were skeptical
- How many times they tried and failed
- What happened each time they failed
- What kind of equipment they were using
- Why it was failing
- How the client's team felt
- The cost of their failure
- What you learned together
- How you learned it

Details like these will add context and make your stories richer. And because many of these issues are the same ones your prospective client is facing, she will see herself in your story. It can seem almost as if you were telling *her* story.

3. Be Entertaining.

Great stories, even dramas, are entertaining, and often the entertainment takes the form of humor. If you have been in sales for any time at all, you already understand the value of humor.

I remember being at a convention in Washington, DC, where the well-known, powerful senator Bob Dole was the keynote speaker. I was expecting a purely political speech. Instead, I heard a stand-up routine. The senator was not a young man, so he used his age for humor. For example, Dole described how when the Roman senator Cicero came up in a debate over a balanced budget amendment, he had said, "I knew Cicero, and Cicero was for a balanced budget." By poking fun at himself, he instantly became more likable and interesting.

As a salesperson, you want to be as likable and interesting as possible. So start collecting funny stories and anecdotes. And think about the potential for humor in your own stories.

- What unexpected problems did you run into with your clients?
- What surprising events occurred?
- What remark did someone make that was totally taken out of context, yet defused a tense situation?

The unexpected is often a good source of humor. See if you can create an amusing anecdote about something that threw you for a loop and weave it into your presentations.

Leave Them Wanting More

Stories are compelling. They move ideas out of the realm of the theoretical and into the real world. They allow you to present your vision and subtly touch upon your values in an entertaining fashion. More important, they lead your clients into a wonderful future, one in which you help them slay their dragons and achieve their goals.

Your clients are dying to hear these stories.

Remember, you are not the hero. You're the heroes' guide, their mentor, and their partner in their journey. Your dream client is the hero in the story. It's his adventure. It's his dragon to slay. You only carry the sword. That's the compelling story line.

FIRST MOVE—DO THIS NOW!

Let's develop a story you are going to need to sell effectively. Write down the story of how you helped one of your largest clients produce better results. Start the story by describing the challenge your client was facing when you first engaged with them. What was wrong? Then describe what they needed. This is the future state they needed to create. Then write the story of how you helped them achieve that future state. Don't leave out the challenges you faced in producing those results together. Your story is more compelling when you explain what it took to create better results.

Practice this story by sharing it with three of your peers. Let them ask you questions so you can add more color to your story.

RECOMMENDED READING

Duarte, Nancy. *Resonate: Present Visual Stories That Transform Audiences.* Hoboken, NJ: Wiley, 2013.

Guber, Peter. *Tell to Win: Connect, Persuade, and Triumph with the Hidden Power of Story.* New York: Crown Business, 2011.

Port, Michael. *Steal the Show: From Speeches to Job Interviews to Deal-Closing Pitches, How to Guarantee a Standing Ovation for All the Performances in Your life.* Boston: Houghton Mifflin Harcourt, 2015.

Chapter 14

DIAGNOSING: THE DESIRE TO UNDERSTAND

It's hard to fix a problem when you don't understand it thoroughly.

—Alice Heiman

THERE'S A CONCEPT IN THE US MILITARY CALLED "THE GROUND truth." It's the idea that while the generals sitting in offices far behind the front lines create plans, the soldiers on the field of battle are the ones who truly understand the battlefield terrain, with all of its horrible threats, challenges, and difficult objectives.

The ground truth is the information gathered on location and it is often very different from what distant planners, experts, and consultants believe it to be. The ground truth—and its tactical realities, obstacles, and unpredictability—is always worse in person than it is on paper. Yet you need to discover the ground truth to perform a real diagnosis on a client company.

The kind of diagnosis I'm talking about requires digging down to the root causes of the company's pain to make your diagnosis. The deeper you dig, the more likely you are to dredge up some uncomfortable truths about what your prospect *really* needs to do to achieve better results. But that's good. Unless you get to the heart of the issues your clients face, you won't be able to create all of the value you are capable of delivering to them.

I'm sure you're familiar with what happens when you haven't discovered the ground truth. Think about it: Have you called on a decision maker, won her business, and then struggled to execute because her description of the problem and the likely solution didn't match the reality in her organization? Or have you ever started working with a client only to discover that the real obstacle to better performance was an issue with the client's people, an unwillingness to change, or a political conflict within his company?

You have probably been trained to call as high up in an organization as possible, moving down only when necessary. That advice is misguided: while you may be *selling* to decision makers, you are *serving* the entire organization. Your diagnosis must include all the people who will be impacted by the decision to move forward with you and your solution. You may be presenting to the C suite, but I promise that you will be executing further down the organizational chart, where the ground truth lives.

Ignoring this truth will lead to serious problems—including unmet expectations and execution difficulties—because *you* will lack a genuine understanding of what is necessary. The groups you find yourself working with will offer resistance because *you* haven't spent time meeting with them to deepen your understanding and to develop trust.

A sound diagnosis, a deep diagnosis, requires that you spend time with staff two or three levels deep in your prospect's company to uncover the ground truth. Only after you have developed this deep understanding of your client should you seek to be understood and offer your ideas and solutions.

THE POWER QUESTION THAT DOUBLES YOUR UNDERSTANDING

One simple question will help you determine the root cause of your prospective client's problems as well as gain a real understanding of what is necessary to produce better results. That question is "Why?"

Suppose your client presents their problem by saying, "We need new equipment to increase our productivity." This is good, because now you know that you need to frame your solution around improved productivity. Still, you haven't discovered the ground truth. You need to ask: "Why do you need to increase your productivity?"

"Because we are failing our customers," the client might answer. "We have already lost one, and we have a few others who aren't happy."

By asking "why" just once, you've moved to the deeper implications. You understand what you really need to do, which is to prevent any more of your client's customers from becoming unhappy and leaving. Now ask why a second time: "Why haven't you changed the equipment and processes before now?"

"Because the finance department has been concerned about costs, and the operations team didn't want to change everything and risk making production even worse."

With this second "why," you learned a lot about how the company operates and which stakeholders may need special handling. This company's management needs to be convinced to spend the necessary money, and the operations team needs a plan for installing new equipment without disrupting production. Focusing on productivity alone would not solve this client's problem, despite what its people initially told you.

GETTING BEYOND THE PRESENTING PROBLEM

Understanding the ground truth helps you to prepare a superior plan and to anticipate and deal with objections. Your solution might not be the best one, but your ability to diagnose the real challenge that your dream client is facing can help you position yourself to win. Maybe you need to be creative and finance the equipment or offer credits or rebates. If you engage the operations team and help them figure out production, perhaps by stockpiling their product until they can switch over to new equipment, you solve another real problem.

HOW TO IMPROVE YOUR DIAGNOSIS

It's not that hard to make an accurate diagnosis if you're aware of and avoid the pitfalls. These include the following:

1. Don't Interpret Your Prospect's Experience through Your Own.

Salespeople are eager to promote their products, services, and solutions because they are confident in their ability to make a difference and because experience tells them that they can succeed. But leading with *your* experience doesn't allow your prospects to go through the buying process, explain their current dissatisfaction, collaborate with you around their needs, and explore options.

Leading with your experience can damage your ability to sell. This is not to say that your experience is unimportant. In fact, your experience is critical to an effective diagnosis. However, we too often view our prospects' problems through our existing solutions and what we have done for other clients. The point of a diagnosis is not to prove that you can push one of your existing solutions on to your prospect. Neither is it to confirm which of your solutions you should sell your client. Rather, it is to learn and discover. Remember, this process is other-oriented.

Proper diagnosis requires that you listen and understand your client's experience. You can apply your own experience later, after you have deepened your understanding.

2. Don't Ignore Your Dream Client's Vision.

It's tempting to filter your client's situations through your own vision of the proper solution, but you would be ignoring the *client's* vision. It's true that clients do not always have the knowledge, expertise, or experience to know how their outcomes can be improved. But when you are open to understanding, you will discover that they often have visions of what they need, and whether they realize it or not, they assess ideas based on those visions.

Brushing aside your prospects' visions of the proper solution is perilous. Don't ignore them. Instead, find out how they see their business results being improved. Even if they're wrong about what is necessary, you must understand what they believe is necessary and work from there. Otherwise, they will feel as if you were trying to shove something down their throats.

3. Consider the Constraints and Obstacles.

It is vital that you uncover the constraints that hinder solutions, whether they be financial, process, external, or other limitations. You must also uncover any obstacles that stand in the way of your developing, selling, implementing, and executing your solution.

It's likely that your competitors didn't understand these constraints when they sold your clients their product or solution. Now your client isn't getting the needed results because the previous salespeople didn't deal with these constraints. You don't want to be the next salesperson to fail because you didn't discover the real obstacles to change.

4. Ask the Difficult Questions.

A sound diagnosis requires asking your client difficult questions. Questions such as the following force a client to face the ground truths in her own company:

- What is the cost of *not* improving performance?
- Why hasn't the problem been solved before?
- Who needs to be on the team to ensure our solutions are approved?
- Who might oppose this solution?

Failing to ask these questions puts your opportunity at risk. Even if your solution is chosen, failure to ask these questions puts the execution of your solution at risk.

Small salespeople ask weak questions. They don't want to bring up big, uncomfortable, challenging issues. For one, they don't know how to deal with those issues. Second, they fear that bringing up tough issues will make their prospects uncomfortable and cost them the deal.

The very best salespeople aren't afraid to ask the tough questions. They "get real"—sometimes very real. They know they are trusted because they aren't afraid to help their clients deal with big, challenging issues. They aren't worried that their client is causing them to stretch because they understand that this is the way to grow. The best salespeople run toward a challenge.

5. Allow Your Dream Client to Teach You How to Win

Opportunities are created, won, or lost in the early stages of the sales process, particularly when you work with your prospects to understand their needs and develop your diagnosis. During this discovery stage, you learn about your prospective clients, while they learn a lot about you and about themselves. This process is critical to creating real value and gaining trust, so make sure you remain as follows:

- **Curious.** Nothing is more crucial to your diagnostic skills than being curious. If you are truly motivated to learn, you will keep digging until you really understand. If you don't care that much, you'll get bored and give up too soon.

- **Patient.** Controlling your desire to instantly share your great ideas and proven solutions is difficult, especially when you recognize the pattern you are seeing—and you've probably seen it many times. But being patient and asking questions will often lead to a much deeper, more nuanced understanding of the situation. That, in turn, will lead to better outcomes for you and your prospect.

By spending the time necessary to understand the needs of the individuals within your prospective client company, you not only gain a better understanding of their real needs, you get an education in what your solution should look like to gain their support.

If you devote the time necessary to understanding your clients' needs, they will teach you what you need to do to win their business, how their business works, and what it takes to enter their world. They will also teach you the language they use to describe their problems, challenges, processes, and systems—language that will allow you to sound as if you were already part of their tribe.

Be curious, be patient, and ask the questions that allow you to dig as deep as is necessary.

ASK AND YOU WILL UNDERSTAND

Once you demonstrate that you care and will go the extra mile to produce added value, your prospective clients will want you to succeed. And once they see that you want to learn, they'll be willing to teach you what you need to know, as long as you ask the right questions.

So ask *all* of the questions that need answering. Don't be shy about asking the hard questions. If you ask them in the right spirit, your prospect will gladly answer. Always remember: good questions create better understanding and therefore more influence.

The real action in the sales process—and in the buying process, for that matter—is in the diagnosis. You don't sell the solution without selling the diagnosis.

FIRST MOVE—DO THIS NOW!

Being excellent at diagnosing your prospective clients' challenges will make you a better salesperson. Make a list of the common challenges your prospective clients have by identifying the presenting problem, the evidence that the problem exists. Then write down next to each of those problems the root cause issue that creates that presenting problem.

RECOMMENDED READING

Paul, Andy. *Amp Up Your Sales: Powerful Strategies That Move Customers to Make Fast, Favorable Decisions.* New York: AMACOM, 2014.

Rackham, Neil. *Major Account Sales Strategy.* New York: McGraw-Hill, 1989.

———. *SPIN Selling.* New York: McGraw-Hill, 1988.

Thull, Jeff. *Mastering the Complex Sale: How to Compete and Win When the Stakes Are High!* Hoboken, NJ: Wiley, 2010.

Chapter 15

NEGOTIATING: CREATING WIN-WIN DEALS

Never negotiate price, negotiate the value the customer will receive.

—Mark Hunter, author of *High-Profit Selling*

SALESPEOPLE TEND TO THINK OF A NEGOTIATION AS A SINGLE event, the "big finish" at the climax of the selling process that results in a signed agreement. But, as I've demonstrated all along in this book, you negotiate throughout the entire process.

If you aren't negotiating, you are either a very lucky salesperson or a very lazy one. If you are negotiating, and you're doing it successfully, you are creating one win-win situation after another.

WHY WIN-WIN?

At first glance, the concept of win-win doesn't make much sense: Why enter into a negotiation hoping to ensure that your "opponent" is delighted with the results? Aren't you supposed to push him back or kick him down so you can grab as much as possible for yourself?

A no-holds-barred approach to negotiations might work if you are planning to make just one sale and then leave the business. Or if your product is so desirable that people are lining up outside your door for a chance to stuff their money into your pockets. (And unless you work for Apple, that probably isn't happening!) If you're in this business for the long haul, though, you'll need clients who respect your ability to create value so much that they will continue to work with you and will recommend you to others. In other words, you need healthy, long-term relationships built on trust and mutual benefit. Being self-oriented is not part of this equation.

This doesn't mean that you should take the opposite tack and give away the store. Salespeople who sell on price alone often negotiate win-lose agreements: these are wins for the customers but losses for the salesperson, who earns just a tiny bit of money for himself and his company. While it can sometimes be tempting to negotiate a win-lose just to close the deal, healthy, long-term relationships cannot benefit the client alone. You must make a profit in order to stay strong enough to deliver value and help your clients achieve better outcomes. And they understand this (even though you may sound self-oriented when you say such things aloud).

In a successful negotiation, there must be no losers. The interests of *all* stakeholders must be maximized—within the client's company and yours—and deals need to provide value to both you and your client.

If you can't devise a win-win agreement, you must walk away. This is the price of being a professional, of being a trusted adviser. You must protect your reputation *and* your client's trust by negotiating to benefit both sides, each and every time.

WHAT HAPPENS WHEN THEY ASK YOU TO CUT YOUR PRICE?

Salespeople face a major challenge when negotiating. We have long trained our clients to expect discounts. Indeed, we have padded our prices in anticipation of the request for a discount and then made pricing concessions accordingly. This practice is now so commonplace, it's routine. Is it any wonder that your clients always ask for a discount?

You've probably received a call like this from your contact at your dream client's company. They love you and your solution, and they know you will produce the best results. Then she drops the bomb: "Of all the finalists, you have the highest price, and to win the business, you'll have to 'sharpen your pencil.'"

You might recognize this as part of the customary dance between buyers and sellers. But the energy you expend negotiating the price and then the discount is better spent helping your clients make the right investment in the results, not in haggling. You serve them better by helping them understand what is possible and selling the value you can create together.

No matter how well you sell throughout the sales process, at some point, you will be asked to discount. You will have to negotiate. But before you decide to negotiate on price alone, try negotiating the value you create.

SHARPEN YOUR VALUE CREATION BEFORE YOU SHARPEN YOUR PENCIL

I was recently copied on an e-mail that a purchasing manager had sent to one of her peers who was heading the committee handling an upcoming deal. The purchasing manager wrote that she would push back on whatever pricing the salesperson proposed, regardless of whether it was high, low, or just right. Apparently, she believed that keeping costs as low as possible created value for her company. She wasn't concerned about *how much* value the proposal created for her company; at least there was no evidence of that in her e-mail. Her approach was, "Make them discount, no matter what."

Not much later, the salesperson involved in this deal, who had already negotiated pricing with the primary stakeholder, submitted the contract. The purchasing manager asked the salesperson for a substantial price reduction.

In reply, the salesperson detailed the value he was creating. He called his primary stakeholder to reiterate this, emphasizing that an underinvestment would not produce the result that his client needed. He focused like a laser beam on the value being created rather than on the price.

And then he politely pushed back. He said he could not agree to any price other than the one he had quoted and still produce the result the client needed. He said he could not accept a lower price and then fail to produce those results, because that would be detrimental to both companies. The person heading up the committee called the purchasing agent, explained the value, and asked for the deal. By pushing back and reminding everyone of the value being created, the salesperson won the deal—and at his quoted price.

Why does this approach work? There are a few things to keep in mind as you enter into a negotiation with your client:

- It is the client's responsibility to get the best possible deal, which prompts the request for a lower price. She's just doing her job; it's what she is expected to do.
- Most of the time, your dream client is willing to invest more money to get the desired result but needs your help in justifying the greater investment.
- The more you can explain and quantify how a greater investment returns greater results, the more likely you are to keep your pricing intact.
- You have to help your contacts sell the deal inside their companies.

When you are asked to defend your price and negotiate a lower price, push back by pointing to the value you are creating. Sharpen your argument for value before sharpening your pencil.

Remind your client that the pricing model you delivered was built on providing *the exact results required*. Point out that there is a difference between price and cost, and highlight what the client stands to lose by investing too little to obtain the required result.

Remind the client why he has not achieved the desired results so far—not enough value has been created. Emphasize that he will not achieve the desired results until that value *is* created. Something has to change. The old negotiating strategy just won't work for him anymore.

HOW TO BE A WIN-WIN NEGOTIATOR

This book is not about tactics. There are excellent books that discuss negotiating philosophies and tactics, including *Getting to Yes: Negotiating Agreement without Giving In* by Roger Fisher and William L. Ury and, one of my favorites, *The StreetSmart Negotiator: How to Outwit, Outmaneuver, and Outlast Your Opponents* by Harry Mills. Both of these books will help you recognize the common tactics employed in negotiations.

Yet a chapter on negotiation raises an important question: Should you use tactics to your advantage or simply study them so you can counter them? I believe that it's a good idea to be familiar with these tactics, but don't wield them to win victory or deal defeat. Remember, you are negotiating with your client (or future client), not outwitting an opponent. If you have developed a strong relationship during the sales process, creating a final agreement will be natural and easy. If the process is adversarial, then you are beginning the relationship on a weak foundation, and you will have to work very hard to create a win-win deal.

Here are four tools to help you be a win-win negotiator:

1. Remember That You Can Walk Away.

You must always negotiate from a position of strength, but you cannot do so unless you are willing to walk away. Either craft a win-win deal, or get up and go.

If the deal is good for your client but not for you, walk. Win-lose deals cost you time and resources that are better dedicated to other clients.

Most of all, they cost you and your team the emotional energy wasted in trying to make something good out of a bad deal.

If, on the other hand, a deal is good for you but bad for your client, you'll need to walk away from that, too. If you don't, you'll eventually lose the client anyway and damage your reputation of being trustworthy. You'll be on your way toward creating a community of disappointed clients who are happy to tell others about their negative experiences with you.

Being willing to walk away from a bad deal gives you a powerful platform for negotiation. You do not have to accept a bad deal, and you never have to try to force someone to accept one. Of course, you can't be in this position if you are dependent on any single deal to make your number. That is why prospecting is so important: a strong, healthy pipeline allows you to walk away from any one deal because there are always plenty more in the offing.

2. Do Not Negotiate Until You Have Been Selected.

Have you ever been in discussion with a potential client only to find the issue of your price raised *before* you are selected? Perhaps you did well during presentations and were immediately told that you needed to sharpen your pencil.

Look out—the negotiations have begun! Or have they?

Some buyers like to pit one salesperson against another in a battle over price. They may or may not share your competitor's prices with you, but they make it clear that you are in a contest over price. If you have not already been selected, you are merely being used as leverage against your competitors. Or maybe your competitor's prices are being used to induce you to lower yours. Either way, if you let the contest shift to price, it shifts away from value.

Protect your pricing by politely insisting on being selected before agreeing to enter into negotiations. If you're asked about price, respond by asking, "Have we been selected?"

If the answer is no, say, "We're happy to negotiate a final agreement, but until you decide that we are the right choice for you, we believe it's premature to start negotiating price. We want to make sure you get the outcomes you need, including the right price."

3. Negotiate Only Once.

Some organizations train their buyers to negotiate more than once, each time pushing the price down and extracting value from you at every step.

First, they make you negotiate with your main contact, and then they bring in the purchasing department for another round of negotiations. Then purchasing brings in the chief financial officer for some more. By spreading out the extraction of value, they pressure you to give up more than you otherwise would. You get sucked in; you become emotionally invested in the deal. They say, "You're so close. If only you could sharpen your pencil a little bit more."

When you negotiate, be certain that it is the final negotiation. Whatever you agree to must be binding. You have to ask, "If we are negotiating price, are you committing to buy upon successfully reaching a number that we both agree will get you the results you need?"

If the answer to that question is not affirmative, you need to ask, "Who else needs to be involved in this negotiation?" Immediately ask to include whoever needs to be involved.

When you negotiate only once, you do what is right for you *and* your dream client. You build optimal value for both parties by creating the best possible deal, only negotiating price at the end.

4. Speak Honestly and Creatively about Sticking Points.

Great salespeople are able to think on their feet, especially when negotiating. However, the ability to think on your feet is no excuse for being unprepared.

Begin preparing for a negotiation by making two lists of critical deal points. One list should contain the points your client needs to create a win for her side, while the other list must detail the points that you need to create a win for you and your team.

Highlight the critical points that are difficult for you as well as those that are problems for your client. Then prepare for an open, honest, and creative dialogue about these sticking points. This is important, for the best negotiations are conversations about how to get through the difficult points together.

Great negotiating is not about winning; it's about creating agreement despite conflicting needs. Be willing to focus on the outcome of a win-win deal, and be resourceful enough to create and discuss new possibilities. Some of that creation will occur at the bargaining table, so come prepared with alternative solutions and ideas.

Before going into a negotiation, meet with thoughtful and creative members of your team to brainstorm other possibilities, potential deal structures, and alternative proposals. Prepare a presentation demonstrating how your ideas allow you and your client to join in a win-win agreement. Focus on ways of overcoming conflicting needs and desires, not just on trade-offs to get the deal done.

And always remember that simple "value claiming" can cause both sides to cling stubbornly to their entrenched positions. When you simply value claim, you are demonstrating a lack of resourcefulness and/or an unwillingness to be creative—the opposite of what you need to be to create value.

When you negotiate with organizations that you intend to work with for years, value claiming isn't a priority. Instead, focus your efforts on being creative enough to arrive at win-win deals that overcome the sticking points.

It's All about Value for Both Parties

You can distinguish yourself as a salesperson by negotiating deals that ensure the client receives the benefit of the bargain, while you profit enough to deliver what you've promised. Your ability to strike a win-win deal, especially when doing so is difficult, will help position you as your client's trusted adviser.

FIRST MOVE—DO THIS NOW!

Justify the delta between your price and your competitors'. Make a list of the things that you do that allow you to produce better results than your primary competitors. Write down three to four bullet points as to why it makes sense for your prospective client to pay more for these differences and how they ensure that they receive the results they need. Use these points when you need to sharpen your value.

RECOMMENDED READING

Cardone, Grant. *Sell or Be Sold: How to Get Your Way in Business and in Life.* Austin, TX: Greenleaf Book Group Press, 2012.

Fisher, Roger, and William L. Ury. *Getting to Yes: Negotiating Agreement without Giving In.* New York: Penguin Books, 2011.

Hunter, Mark. *High-Profit Selling: Win the Sale without Compromising on Price.* New York: American Management Association, 2012.

Malhotra, Deepak, and Max H. Bazerman. *Negotiation Genius: How to Overcome Obstacles and Achieve Brilliant Results at the Bargaining Table and Beyond.* New York: Bantam, 2007.

Chapter 16

BUSINESS ACUMEN: UNDERSTANDING BUSINESS AND CREATING VALUE

The real decision makers—the leaders in business—care about innovation, outcomes and managing risk. Know your client's industry and their customers; then bring insight and expertise that helps them with strategy, game-changing business value and managing risk.

—Tony Hughes, author of *The Joshua Principle*

MANY SALESPEOPLE FAIL TO CREATE OR WIN NEW OPPORTUNI-
ties because they don't know enough about business. They mistakenly believe that it's enough to know their product or service to have just a tiny bit of sales acumen—mostly a rehearsed script for overcoming objections.

Product knowledge alone might have been enough in the past, but today your dream clients aren't interested in hiring just a salesperson. They want someone who can help them solve their business challenges. They are looking for a partner who will help them visualize a better future and guide them toward it. A salesperson who just recites product features and benefits is no more valuable than a good Web site—and less valuable than a really good YouTube video. Your dream clients want a trusted adviser.

To become a trusted adviser, you must be able to dispense excellent, sound advice. And to do that, you must have business acumen: an understanding of general business principles and the ability to use them to make thoughtful business decisions in your particular field. Business acumen forms the core of value creation for your clients.

ACUMEN BUILDS VALUE

In the not-too-distant past, the teaching of sales skills was limited to prospecting, storytelling, and closing, with an emphasis on closing. These are what we call *first-generation sales skills*. Then, as the profession changed due to evolving economic conditions, salespeople were trained to diagnose their clients' more complex needs so they could differentiate their offerings from their competitors'. They were taught to use the value they create as a primary negotiating tool. These are *second-generation sales skills*.

Although both first- and second-generation skills are necessary, they are no longer enough for sales success. The rising prominence of value creation has triggered a need for a new set of skills. Today, you must also know how business works. You must truly understand market strategy, unique value propositions, financial metrics, and more, all *third-generation sales skills*.

The new reality is that you can no longer be "just" a salesperson; you must also be a business generalist. Business acumen helps you create opportunities by identifying areas where value can be created—value that solves real business problems and creates a competitive advantage. You are comfortable discussing profitability, metrics, throughput, ROI, and any number of other financial measurements. You can also discuss execution with your clients' operations staff and examine complex ideas and details with their technical teams. You can even review compliance and legal issues with your clients' procurement and risk-management teams. To be fluent in all of these areas, you don't need to become an expert, but you do need to develop an understanding of business in general and your client's business in particular.

As you do discovery work, your business acumen will provide you with the necessary insight to ask the right questions at the right time. And when you build a proposal, it will help you think like a businessperson— like the person who decides whether or not to buy what you're selling.

HOW TO IMPROVE YOUR BUSINESS ACUMEN

Business acumen takes time and effort to acquire, but it does not necessarily require money or an Ivy League MBA degree. Here are seven ways to improve your business acumen, six of which cost almost nothing more than conscious and consistent effort:

1. Read Business Books and Magazines.

The first step in acquiring business acumen is to master the fundamental concepts and vocabulary of business. Fortunately, both topics have been thoroughly researched and written about, and information is available at a shockingly low price.

Business books take years to write and represent thousands of hours of research. They contain the valuable experience of practitioners and theorists, including the stories of their successes and mistakes. The cost of a business book averages only about twenty-five dollars. If the author spent a full work year writing it (2,080 hours), you are paying a little over one cent per hour for his or her work. That's an amazing amount of value for the price!

Read widely and from a variety of fields. Read books on marketing, management, leadership, and even a book or two on finance. Read biographies of business leaders to understand the challenges they faced, how they thought about those challenges, and the choices they made to overcome them.

In addition to business books, read magazines such as *Fast Company, Harvard Business Review, Bloomberg Businessweek, Forbes, Fortune,* and *Inc.,* all of which will introduce you to useful ideas. Over time, you will become familiar with the language of business and begin to understand many of the major themes, ideas, trends, and issues.

My good friend John Spence has been reading three to five business books a week for decades. He can speak knowledgeably with anyone on any business-related subject, a major reason that many Fortune 500 companies hire him to speak or train their teams.

Download my list of recommended reading at www.theonlysales guide.com.

2. Read Nonfiction Books That Have Nothing to Do with Business.

As much as business books and magazines will help you develop your business acumen, you can gain even more insight by reading nonbusiness books. Reading widely can provide you with plenty of situational knowledge and a lot of interesting and useful ideas that will help you make connections.

You would do well to pick up books like *The Checklist Manifesto: How to Get Things Right* or *Better: A Surgeon's Notes on Performance,* both by Atul Gawande. Neither volume would be considered a business book, yet each teaches valuable lessons easily applied to businesses of all kinds.

You would also benefit greatly by reading Howard Bloom's *The Genius of the Beast: A Radical Re-Vision of Capitalism* or his magnum opus, *The Lucifer Principle: A Scientific Expedition into the Forces of History.* Both books can teach you more about sales and marketing than many other books you might read, even though neither is specifically about those topics. Instead, they are about culture and the deep needs of human beings. They're part science, part history, part psychology, and part marketing.

Choose nonfiction books that interest you. Even books about topics that seem to be far afield, like history and art, can be very useful. I promise that you will find something that applies to your sales job and some concept that helps you better understand business.

3. Find Company Tutors.

Your company almost certainly offers free training and has resources aimed at employee development. But one often overlooked resource is your coworkers—in your own and other departments. Most people would love to help you understand their areas of expertise by showing off what they know. Company tutors may not be formally offered, but, hey, you're in sales. You know there is always a way to get what you need.

Need a better understanding of financial reports? Go to your finance and accounting departments and ask staffers to walk you through your dream client's financial reports and tell you what they see. Once the staffers recognize that they are the teachers and you are an eager student, you might have a tough time escaping their lessons!

Need help understanding how people in operations think about a certain business challenge? How about procurement, marketing, or executive management? Ask people in those departments in your company to tell you about what they do and how they think. Request reading material that will give you a higher level of understanding. Then ask them to join you for lunch to discuss what you've learned. Not only will you be gaining valuable business acumen, you'll also be creating relationships with people whose help you may need later on.

Find and develop tutors. You can reciprocate by giving them an education in how sales works. Believe me, they will be thrilled to teach and to learn.

4. Get Mentors.

You probably have family members, neighbors, friends, members of your church or synagogue, or acquaintances who have expertise in some area of business. Most likely, these people would be happy to share their knowledge and understanding with you, if you ask.

Ask these people to mentor you and educate you in their areas of expertise. They will probably be flattered and excited to help you. Find two or three who know about a certain area of business and rotate your Friday lunch hour between these new mentors. Take notes on what you've learned from their experiences, their most important ideas, and their advice for learning more.

Some time ago, I was having trouble understanding debt ratios and sustainable growth rates. My neighbor happened to be a chief financial officer, so I asked him to review the spreadsheets with me. Not only did he teach me how to look at cash flow and sustainable growth, but he also revised all of my spreadsheets for me and taught me how to set them up for the next analysis.

Don't be shy about reaching out for help. There are always people who are willing to educate you. You just have to ask.

5. Let the Client Teach You His Business.

Your clients know their businesses backward and forward and will be more than happy to teach you about them.

A client may be able to share with you many aspects of the company's operations, including hiring employees (human resources); competing in markets (strategy, marketing); serving customers (operations, customer service); financial results and concerns (accounting, finance, strategy); and managing and leading employees (management and leadership).

Learning from your clients about their businesses is a working person's MBA. The practical knowledge and experience you gain can do much to help you create value for your dream clients.

In addition, your clients will be grateful that you are trying to understand their businesses and improve your general business acumen. That's because they know that your improved understanding can help them produce better and faster results.

Make a list of questions that you'd like to ask your clients about their businesses. Invite members of client teams to lunch and ask what they believe is important about their businesses.

I spent the better part of ten years asking my clients to teach me their businesses. I asked about every area of their operations and told them very directly that I wanted to understand the business as well as they did. Later, after years of asking questions, I was able to ask questions that demonstrated my own developing expertise in their organization.

6. Write Down What You Learn.

Keeping track of the lessons you learn is a great way to educate yourself. Make notes about important ideas, where and when you became acquainted with them, and riff on how your new knowledge might be useful to you and your clients.

The act of writing not only helps you remember, but it also encourages you to think about what you have learned. And thinking, of course, deepens your understanding.

If you take notes on your computer or tablet, go back through your notes, highlight different passages, and add your comments and thoughts. Doing so will bring you greater clarity and help you remember what you've learned. Reviewing what you have learned once a quarter will not only make what you learned actionable, it will also help you generate new ideas.

7. Get a Formal Education.

This is the only one of the seven ideas that costs more than a few bucks—and, if you are willing to devote the necessary money, time, and mental energy, the university experience can be fun, exciting, and extremely rewarding in building your business acumen. Consider an MBA, extension classes, certificate programs, a master's degree in some aspect of business, or even a bachelor's degree.

Before you even show up for your first class, you will be given a reading list. So by the time you get there, you'll have had time to think about what you've read and be able to discuss the topics covered with your classmates. There is nothing more invigorating than banging around ideas with a group of thoughtful people who have just read the same books you have.

Although business author and speaker Tom Peters has been known to rail against MBAs, I believe that getting an MBA is a great exercise in learning. In the future, you will see a lot more salespeople with MBAs because sales requires higher and higher levels of business acumen.

Can't afford an MBA? Don't worry. Your local community college offers classes in business, finance, accounting, writing, and a host of other subjects, all of which can enhance your business acumen.

And, of course, if you truly work the first six ways of improving your business acumen, you'll have the equivalent of an informal MBA.

Know More Than What You Are Selling

As we have progressed from simply selling products to selling solutions and the improvement and acceleration of business, the skills required to succeed in sales have evolved. Today, if you want to be effective, you need to be a great businessperson.

Yet business acumen is still rare in sales. We spend too much time worrying about product knowledge, technical knowledge, and sales acumen when we should be focusing on business acumen.

Your business knowledge and experience are tremendous assets. The more you develop these assets, the better your sales results will be. Whether your education is formal or informal, the ROI will be tremendous.

You create value by helping people further their business goals. Salespeople need to be good businesspeople. Why? Because business acumen is the new sales acumen.

FIRST MOVE—DO THIS NOW!

Select one public company that interests you. It might be one of your dream clients, but it doesn't have to be. Go to finance.yahoo.com or www.google.com/finance and download their latest annual report. Read the annual report, especially the chairperson's letter to shareholders. Also read the risk assessment to understand what trends or events may harm their results and how they think about those issues. If you want a good company to start with, choose General Electric.

RECOMMENDED READING

Dixon, Matthew, and Brent Adamson. *The Challenger Sale: Taking Control of the Customer Conversation*. New York: Portfolio, 2011.

Hughes, Tony J. *The Joshua Principle: Leadership Secrets of Selling*. Portland, OR: BookBaby, 2013.

Kaufman, Josh. *The Personal MBA: Master the Art of Business*. New York: Portfolio, 2010.

Malcolm, Jack. *Bottom-Line Selling: The Sales Professional's Guide to Improving Customer Profits*. Seattle: Booktrope, 2011.

Spence, John. *Awesomely Simple: Essential Business Strategies for Turning Ideas into Action*. San Francisco: Jossey-Bass, 2009.

Chapter 17

CHANGE MANAGEMENT: BUILDING CONSENSUS AND HELPING OTHERS CHANGE

The real key to change management lies in mind-set management.

—Gerhard Gschwandtner, publisher of *Selling Power* magazine

WHAT YOU SELL IS GOING TO CHANGE SOMETHING IN YOUR CLI-ent's business, perhaps in a very big way.

Implementing this change might sound easy. For example, just install the new software, train the tech folks, and hand over the manual. But your client's business is not just a company name; it is a complex collection of people with different needs, wants, and demands, many of which may conflict. In order to make your offering valuable, all these people must work together. That's why building a consensus within your client's company is a very necessary, people-oriented process.

In most cases, you have to manage the change by moving individuals, teams, and even entire organizations from their current state to a better state. It's a demanding task that requires all of the traits and abilities you learned about in previous chapters: optimism, initiative, resourcefulness, determination, caring, empathy, emotional intelligence, communication, influence, closing, business acumen, diagnosing, storytelling, and negotiation. That's why the discussion of change management comes last, because you will need every tool you've acquired up to this point to do so.

WHY DO THEY TAKE THE BLUE PILL?

There is a great scene in the movie *The Matrix* that sets up the film's whole premise. Morpheus, the guide, offers Neo, the seeker, a choice of two pills: one red and one blue. Neo is told that if he takes the red pill, his eyes will be opened to the ugly truth of reality, a truth he will no longer be able to avoid. If he takes the blue pill, he will remain in the world he already knows and will continue to maintain his present beliefs, even if they are lies.

The red pill represents the uncertainty that comes with change; the blue pill represents the status quo. When you sell, you are, in a sense, asking your clients to choose between the red and the blue pills. They know that if they take the red pill, they will have to face the unknown and make the improvements that have been difficult or impossible to achieve in the past. Change is a potential disruption to businesses, carrying the risk of failure in a very visible way. This is one major reason why there is always so much resistance to the changes you propose to your clients' organizations.

To persuade them to embrace change, you must help them confront the truth of their situations and visualize a better future. Acknowledge that this change will come with pain, but that on the other side of that pain lies a better place. Help them deal with internal company politics and reinforce the belief that they will receive the outcomes you have sold them.

ENLISTING THE SUPPORT OF THE DOUBTERS

There is an excellent chance that some "blue pill" stakeholders in your client's company will put up a lot of resistance to your solution. Indeed, they may go to battle with your supporters to prevent implementation.

You need to get these doubters on your side. It's not enough to have the backing of those who support your solution. Without the assistance of those who oppose change, your solution will not produce a better outcome. It cannot, because the doubters will drag their feet and try to wait you out. They will work against your efforts, making sure that every misstep and every mistake, regardless of how small it is, is greeted with loud complaints.

If you have ever moved forward without gaining the support of the teams you need, you know how badly this story can end for you and your client. Never ignore those who oppose you, and never try to steamroll your change through. Instead, identify those who stand in opposition and build internal teams that can sell the idea of exchanging the status quo for something better.

To do so, you'll need to arm these teams with powerful arguments, which means you'll have to identify the areas of conflict within the company and then build solutions that minimize or eliminate the disagreements.

A VERY SHORT COURSE IN STAKEHOLDER ANALYSIS

We sell in a world where more and more decisions are made by consensus. More people are engaged in the process, and we need everyone to come along with us as we make change. Or, at least, we need them to stand down and allow the change to happen. In most deals, a decision to move forward requires something north of a majority, and almost any single person can veto your proposal.

The more complex the solution you propose, the more likely it is that many stakeholders will be affected. By the same token, the more important to your dream client's success your solution is, the greater the number of people involved in the process.

There are many approaches to managing the complex web of relationships found in every company, from target to close. Perhaps the most effective tool is a stakeholder analysis: a profile of the various people, teams, divisions, and silos involved. What follows is a short course in completing an analysis.

1. Figure Out Who Decides, Formally and Informally.

Begin by identifying all the contacts within your client's company who are likely to be on the buying committee. This sounds simple, but it's not always easy.

Ideally, you'll identify the power sponsors, the people with influence who support your solution. The easiest way to find them is to ask your contact a simple question: "Whom do we need on our team if we want to get the green light for this project?"

There are other stakeholders to consider. These people may not be on the buying committee, but their cooperation is almost always necessary to ensure that your solution produces the promised results. They often hold the real power to choose the solution and can certainly tell you what is really going on within the company. To find them, ask your contact: "Who will be affected when we implement the solution?"

Then there are the invisible influences: those within the company who have no formal or direct connection to your solution but are highly respected or politically powerful and can sway a decision. They are often difficult to identify, which means you must spend sufficient time with your contacts and pay close enough attention during your sales interactions to figure out who influences whom.

You might need to make suggestions to help your contact think of all of the necessary people. You can say: "We normally find that if we bring in the operations staff and the IT people early in the process, we are more likely to understand their needs and receive their buy-in. This makes it a lot easier to get things done. Whom should we get on board early?"

2. Figure Out What They Need.

The better you understand the needs and fears of various stakeholders, the more likely you are to deliver whatever is necessary to obtain their support.

For example, your client's leadership team may support your initiative. But then you find that someone way down the organizational chart needs you to alter your solution so it fits with her current work flow. Selling without knowing this—and without the support of everyone on the chart—could lead to failure.

You might find that some technical specification in your solution conflicts with a feature your customer's IT people care deeply about. Or maybe the finance department is trying to create breathing room when it comes to cash flow, and your deal hinges upon giving credit terms outside of your normal practices.

There may be someone within the organization who is hell-bent on taking credit for some new initiative and who withholds support unless you make changes that allow *her* to take credit for them. You may not like these kinds of internal politics, but they come with the territory.

Further, you will inevitably run into someone you need who has a long-standing, close relationship with your competitor. It doesn't matter that your competitor is failing; this stakeholder wants to support his friend.

Carefully consider all the stakeholders and their biases and preferences. Some will be supporters, maybe even power sponsors, who want you to succeed and will do all they can to help you. All you have to do for them is provide the information they need to champion you within the company.

As for those who oppose you, figure out why. Do they have their own horses in the race that will lose if you win? Will their power be diminished by your solution? Are they against change simply because it makes them feel uncomfortable?

Finally, don't overlook the neutral stakeholders: those who will not go out of their way to support you or block you. These contacts need to be managed, too, to prevent opposing stakeholders from turning them against you.

3. Work through Conflicts and Constraints.

Once you have identified all the players, lay out their conflicting needs and constraints so you can strategize with your team. Some of your client's stakeholders might want a certain solution because it helps them get the results *they* need, while others may want something very different because it serves *their* needs better. Once you've figured out where these conflicts and constraints lie, you can work toward building a solution agreeable to all groups. It's not easy to do this, but if you don't, the stakeholder with the most power will most likely obtain the solution she wants, right or wrong. That may seem great if the stakeholder happens to be your power sponsor. But if you win solely because your champion has the most power, your solution will be hobbled down the line by resistance from the losing stakeholders.

4. Don't Focus on the Heights.

Efforts to implement change often fail because salespeople focus too much on finding the person or people with the authority to seal a deal.

As I noted earlier, most of us were taught to start as high as possible in the client company's organization to ensure that we connect with the person vital to binding a deal. This might have been good advice in the past, but today more and more companies are making decisions based on a consensus of the stakeholders affected by the purchase. This means that the power to decide is often spread across several departments and multiple levels. Thus, the real power often resides farther down the organizational chart than it used to. So don't ignore the many stakeholders who are not at the top of the food chain.

HOW TO MANAGE CHANGE

Now that you've performed your stakeholder analysis, you're ready to begin managing the change. Here's how:

1. Identify and Build Your Team.

It is no longer enough to identify and sell only to the economic decision maker, the person paying for your solution. Neither is it enough to find a decision influencer and get him on your side. Instead, you need to develop a coalition of decision makers, decision influencers, and stakeholders who will help you sell the idea of change and then help you execute it once you win. In other words, you need to build a team.

As you consider the players in the organization, figure out whom you need on your team. Who will benefit most from your solution? Who has the greatest political power in the organization? Who has the most influence over other decision makers, decision influencers, and stakeholders? Who is passionate enough about your idea to sell your ideas when you are not there?

Gather these people and create a team that will help you build and sell your case for change.

2. Identify the Obstacles to Change.

Many deals evaporate because you've underestimated obstacles. One of the biggest obstacles consists of people within the company who oppose your change. Use your stakeholder analysis to identify all those who oppose change and their reasons, including people who are open to your solution but closed to the idea of change itself. The status quo has many defenders; the case against risk is always strong and easily made. The defenders know that something is wrong, but the status quo is the devil they know.

Too often, salespeople sell to those most receptive to their offering, ignoring opportunities to win over the stakeholders who have reservations. Unfortunately, avoidance isn't a consensus-building strategy. You must be diligent in identifying those who oppose your initiative, engage them, and learn why they are standing in your way. Only then can you win them over.

3. Deal with Conflicting Interests.

While change might be valuable in one area of your client's company, it might create difficulty in another. So it's not just the human obstacles you need to consider. Identify and handle the technical obstacles as well, and the sooner, the better.

Too often we present our solutions before we have identified all of the technical challenges and conflicting interests and constructed a plan for handling them. We leave the client with a wonderful presentation, a terrific solution, and a long list of unresolved concerns.

Make a list of the conflicts, technical and human, and devise solutions to all of them long before you make your presentation to the stakeholders. Strive to get agreement from all who would be negatively affected by your change initiative *before* you present.

Which stakeholders do you need to meet with to solicit their objections and mitigate any problems your solution may cause them? Who on your team can help you gain their support or ask them to stand down?

4. Build and Sell the Case for Killing the Status Quo.

No one wants to kill the status quo only to replace it with something similar. It is not worth the work, the disruption, or stepping off the cliff into the unknown. To build support for your proposed change, you must convincingly demonstrate why the status quo is lacking and even dangerous, and how your solution will create a better future. Use your storytelling skills to sell that bright, shiny future.

Build your ROI analysis in financial and human terms. Answer "What's in it for me?" for as many parties as possible. Sell your story and your ROI to the stakeholders who support you. Convince the stakeholders who oppose you that your change will work for them, too. Make the case that the status quo is, in fact, riskier than change. Make it compelling.

5. Play Politics.

Every organization is riddled with politics, which means you'll have to learn and play the company's political games. While this can be ugly and messy, it's absolutely necessary.

To lessen conflict, give opponents something they want. Modify parts of your offer to win over enough people that you can execute the deal. You might have to court the opponents and nurture these relationships to build trust, especially when what you sell comes with a healthy serving of blood, sweat, and tears (on their part).

All of these ideas must be applied to your own organization as well. Sometimes moving a client from no action to action requires that you change something in your own camp. You may need to go to your team and ask for changes to the way a product is delivered, the time frame in which it's delivered, or additional resources. You may have to ask for special credit terms, a single point of contact dedicated to the client, or help with a clause in a contract. You need consensus inside your own organization, and the same strategies and tactics that work with clients work internally.

Become a master politician so you can provide the catalyst for change and then manage it. Often, this is the real heart of change management.

Overcome the Challenges to Change

Making changes in any company is difficult. You have to go into every deal with your eyes wide open, knowing that you will encounter many types of resistance—and some of it may lie within your own company.

Your job is to create and sell a compelling case for change and then manage and lead that change. Identify the status quo and build an awareness of risks associated with maintaining it. And remember that every time you identify a threat to your clients' businesses, you identify another opportunity to create a better outcome.

Great salespeople do more than sell their products or services. Great salespeople create and sell a case for change. Then they manage and lead that change.

FiRST MOVE—DO THIS NOW!

Identify all the opportunities in your pipeline where you only have one stakeholder engaged with you around the process of change. Call and schedule an appointment with your primary contact to pitch bringing in the other stakeholders who are going to be involved in any decision to move forward. Then start booking meetings with all of the stakeholders whose help you are going to need to make your real change.

RECOMMENDED READING

Adamson, Brent, and Matthew Dixon. *The Challenger Customer: Selling to the Hidden Influencer Who Can Multiply Your Results*. New York: Portfolio, 2015.

Heath, Chip, and Dan Heath. *Switch: How to Change Things When Change Is Hard*. Waterville, ME: Thorndike, 2011.

Kotter, John P. *Leading Change*. Boston: Harvard Business Review Press, 2012.

Chapter 18

LEADERSHIP: PRODUCING RESULTS WITH AND THROUGH OTHERS

You have to lead yourself first, then your team and finally your client's team. No one makes you a leader. You step up and earn the right to lead.

—John Spence, author of *Awesomely Simple*

YOU PROBABLY THINK OF YOURSELF PRIMARILY AS A SALESPER- son and not as a leader. You're out in the field doing the heavy lifting, not sitting in a conference room making plans or giving speeches to the many people you lead. You may not even want to be a leader. But if you are going to sell and produce the outcomes you promise your clients, you'll have to take a leadership role.

Leadership, as it pertains to the philosophy of this book, is the act of determining a course of action to produce extraordinary results and then employing the resources of others to make it happen. To do this, you call upon your storytelling, negotiating, and change-management skills, all the while demonstrating your unswerving accountability. (Once again, you'll notice how everything in this book weaves together in an interconnected web of attributes and skills that build upon each other.)

As a great salesperson, you lead from the front, guiding your team and the client's cross-functional team. When a problem, challenge, or obstacle pops up, you are the first person to deal with it, regardless of how unpleasant it might be. When an opportunity is identified, you are the first to exploit it. This is what a leader does.

You're a strategic orchestrator. Like an orchestra conductor, your job is to keep everybody on the same page in order to produce the best result. You will lead others with far greater knowledge of their particular responsibilities than you can ever hope to possess. The conductor doesn't play violin well enough to sit first or second chair—but he or she knows the roles of those violinists well enough to deploy their talents where and when they are necessary. The people on your team who execute and deliver know far more about what they do than you do, but you have to lead them nonetheless.

That's OK, because you are providing the vision, the direction. They'll handle the details. Remember, you own outcomes, and they own the transactions (as you learned in chapter 9 on accountability).

NO ONE MAKES YOU A LEADER

Leadership is never handed to you as a salesperson. No authority figure walks over, taps you on the shoulder, and says, "Congratulations. You are now a leader." There is no great ceremony at which someone in your company gives you permission to lead, and it's likely that no one will teach you how to lead. What makes you a leader is your decision to take responsibility and to act on that decision, no matter your position on the organizational chart. You become a leader simply by behaving like a leader, by owning the responsibility for the outcome you sell.

Choose to be a leader. Take responsibility for producing results, for helping your clients create the outcomes you sold them. And don't worry about someone complaining that you're leading. I promise that no one will fight you for the leadership role, especially when you have to overcome difficult challenges. Some people will try to snatch the credit once a successful outcome is obtained, but they will not fight you for the heavy lifting that gets you there. Many will run and hide when the train comes off the tracks, seeking to absolve themselves of responsibility.

You won't run and hide. You will engage. You will lead. And others will follow you and help you because you are out front, leading the charge.

MANAGING THE "DEPARTMENT OF SALES PREVENTION"

One of the most difficult sales you will ever make is to your own company. If you have sold for any time at all, I know you hate this immutable truth of selling. Hating that this is true does nothing to make it less true, though, and it does even less to change the reality that you have to do as much work selling inside your company as you do selling inside your dream client's company.

Your own company is full of skeptics who don't believe they can produce the outcomes your dream client needs for you to win the business. That's because the status quo isn't just entrenched in your client's company; it's also deeply embedded in your own. This resistance to change, this unwillingness to stretch, creates what I lovingly refer to as the Department of Sales Prevention, headed by a vice president of We Can't. There's one (or more) in every sales organization.

You know how it works. Your solution is nearly complete. Your dream client needs you to make a few tweaks to the way you do things so that it exactly fits their work flow and allows them to gain the consensus of some on their team. You bring back the modifications, and your team tells you, "We can't."

The deal you are working on requires you to make some investment. Maybe you have to hire an additional person to work on the account, even though their billing won't justify that expense for months. Or maybe you need to buy supplies outside of what you have on hand to ensure that the clients get the outcome they need. This requires a little leap of faith that the investment is going to work in your favor sooner rather than later. You are confident that it will. Your company's leadership doesn't share your confidence. They haven't been engaged with the client, and they weren't in the room during the dozens of sales calls you had with your dream client. Their answer? "We can't."

Often, your own leadership team has to be persuaded to adopt your vision of what is possible and necessary. Instead of looking for ways to innovate, to create new value that can later be rolled out to even more clients, the folks in your Department of Sales Prevention will reflexively respond with, "No. We can't do that."

This is where your leadership is required. No, you do not have the formal authority to lead within your own organization, but don't let that stop you. Lead internally by using all of the skills you apply in selling to clients. Offer a vision of a better future and build consensus around that vision. Play politics if you have to. Be bold enough to ask for commitments from people over whom you have no authority. Stay the course until you finally get what you want, just as you do when winning deals.

Let's get one other thing straight when it comes to leadership: The fact that there is resistance within your own company is the reality you are faced with sometimes as a salesperson. It's not something to get upset about. It isn't something that you can whine about or wish away. There is nothing easy about selling today, and this reality means that you have to step, lead, and move people into the future—sometimes kicking and screaming.

NEVER *BLAME* YOUR COMPANY—LEAD IT

If something goes wrong and you can't deliver the promised results to your client, you can't blame your own company. Doing so will not absolve you of responsibility for the failure, even if your company was obviously to blame.

Weak salespeople are not leaders. Weak salespeople blame their company, believing that this somehow makes them less responsible. But as far as their clients are concerned, the salesperson *is* the company! The salesperson is who sold them, not the salesperson's company. The salesperson was on-site, having meetings, diagnosing their needs, and building consensus.

You are never going to hear a customer say, "It's OK. We're not mad at you for failing us. We're mad at your company. We'll buy from you again when you work at another company." Look, if you couldn't get them the result this time at this company, why should they believe you'll do a better job at another company? You'll face similar challenges in your next sales job. It's inevitable.

Your dream clients hired you to help them produce a result. They expect you to lead your team to produce that result. If changes are necessary, they expect you to lead your team in making those changes. *You* made the promise, and *you* are responsible for delivering. Period.

You sold results, and that's what a leader delivers.

LEAD YOUR OWN TEAM

Your team needs a leader, and there's no one better to fill that role than you. Meet with your team members—including your management team, operations managers, accounting and IT departments—to give them a vision. When they struggle, act on the belief that they are doing their best. Assume good intentions. Instead of being critical or judgmental, spend time understanding their world and the obstacles that prevent them from executing. Your role is to help them succeed, not to blame them for failing.

Once you understand the obstacles your team members face, explain to them what is at stake for your client as well as what is at stake for your company. If the problems are being generated on the client's side, lead by intervening on behalf of your team and explaining to your client's team members how the actions that they are taking (or not taking) might be preventing your team from executing.

If your team is missing internal resources necessary to serve your client, work your internal relationships to supply what's needed. Your team might need more time, more money, more people, or more support from the leadership inside your company. You are responsible for making sure that they have what they need or helping them to acquire it. Now you are reminded why you need to be resourceful, influential, and why you need to build consensus; these attributes and skills are necessary inside both your company and your client's company.

Give your team firm leadership, and it will go out of its way to help you deliver.

CLEAR THE WAY

There is a great scene in the movie *Patton* where General George S. Patton is racing across Italy in an attempt to beat the British general Bernard Montgomery to Messina. Patton's soldiers are trying to cross a bridge, but a donkey pulling a cart is blocking it. The donkey, proving its reputation for stubbornness, refuses to move.

Eager to capture Messina before Montgomery does, Patton walks up to see what's preventing his men from acting upon his command to get to the destination. Upon discovering the obstacle, the general pulls out his famed pearl-handled pistol and shoots the donkey. Patton then orders his men to push the donkey and cart over the side of the bridge, and his team reaches Messina ahead of Montgomery.

Obstacle removed. Objective achieved.

You, too, will encounter obstacles that slow or halt your team. Some of these obstacles may be as stubborn as a donkey. Maybe your client has created these obstacles in the form of new pricing demands or service-level agreements, or by allowing stakeholders entrenched in the status quo to delay needed changes. Perhaps your own company has placed obstacles in your way by demanding unreasonable credit terms, pushing out delivery dates, or letting operational folks drag their feet because the outcome you sold is going to stretch them a little.

It doesn't matter where the obstacles come from. Your role as a leader is to deal with stubborn donkeys and clear the road so that your team can race to deliver the promised results. You don't need to act with the same cruelty that Patton did; he was literally at war. But you do need to act with as much vigor and commitment.

This is why you must always lead from the front: you need to be the first one to spot the donkeys so you can deal with them right away.

HOW TO IMPROVE YOUR ABILITY TO LEAD OTHERS

Ask any leader, and they'll tell you that it is difficult to lead under the best of circumstances. They'll explain how ineffective the use of force is when leading a team, and they will tell you that they wish they had more influence. Great leaders always choose persuasion over force. They know that they are salespeople selling a vision and asking for the commitment of action to bring that vision to life.

Great leaders will also tell you that what keeps them up at night isn't the threat of their competitors; it's the risk of failing the people who they have the honor to lead.

You've made it this far into the book, and that means there is a great likelihood that you've got the stuff to be a great leader. Sadly, most people who buy a book like this don't make it past the first couple of chapters. You have distinguished yourself!

Here are some tools that will help you strengthen your leadership skills:

1. Read about and Study Leadership.

Few sales organizations focus on training and development to help their salespeople become leaders. This serious oversight means that you have to train and develop yourself, and reading is a great way to start.

I like to read books by practitioners of leadership—leaders who were faced with challenges that seemed insurmountable—such as Sir Ernest

Henry Shackleton, President George Washington, and General George Patton. As you read, it's easy to distill leaders' stories into lists of ideas and attributes. If you don't like to read biographies, or if you don't like distilling the lessons yourself, choose a book that has a number in the title, which means that someone else has captured the stories and distilled the lessons for you (see **Recommended Reading**).

Ideas will pop into your head as you read; write them down. Make notes about the skills and attributes of leadership, and collect stories illustrating how they come into play in your business. Be sure to write down examples of leadership failures and think about which leadership skills and attributes might have prevented those disasters. This exercise will ingrain these lessons in your mind, and you will find yourself thinking of ways you can solve your own leadership challenges.

Also study the great leaders in your organization. These leaders may not have the formal titles you think of when you think of leaders. Look for the people whom get things done because people willingly follow them. Identify those who people work for and with because they are getting something more than just a paycheck. Notice how they communicate with the people they lead. Watch for clues that help you understand what the leader does that makes her worth following. Does she care about her people? Does she provide them with a compelling mission and vision? Does she frame their work as something so important as to provide meaning and purpose to the daily grind?

2. Learn to Own the Outcome.

Leaders always take responsibility, whether or not things go well. Even if a failure is due to unforeseen circumstances or to the client's omissions or errors, a leader takes responsibility.

Learning to own the outcome means accepting responsibility for helping your client achieve the outcome you sold. It also means tackling the biggest problems. Don't hesitate to lead because you fear you will be on your own: good leaders naturally attract dedicated followers. In fact, the very act of leading is how you *create* followers—people who join your effort because they, too, want you and your solution to succeed. When you jump right in to do the heavy lifting, you earn followers.

I once had a client who failed to get the outcome that I had sold to his company. Dysfunctional members of his leadership team were responsible for the failure. The people in leadership roles in his company were very aggressive, and they were very disrespectful to the people on my team. Instead of working to help us achieve the goal their company needed, they belittled and badgered my people, hammering them to produce better results while doing everything they could to prevent our success. The company needed to change the way it worked with us, or achieving the results would be impossible.

I could have very easily absolved myself of any responsibility, blamed my client for the failure, and moved on. Instead, I owned the outcome, which meant I took responsibility for dealing with the client's team and his constraints. Needless to say, the conversations weren't pleasant. I didn't make many friends when I suggested that his team was the only thing standing in the way of better results. But they took my advice and changed, and together we produced a better outcome than we would have had I not taken a leadership role.

You learn to lead by stepping into the breach. You learn to lead by tackling the tough issues from which most people run away. You will quickly find yourself in over your head—and that is where leaders are made.

3. Lead from the Front.

Leadership is found where the action is—at the front—with leaders helping out, rallying the people, and securing the necessary resources.

Do not lead from behind a desk. Go where the action is and make your presence felt. Stand shoulder to shoulder with your clients during difficult times. The same is true when your own team struggles. You must be on the front lines with your soldiers as they battle their fiercest challenges.

Remember, you created and sold the vision. When problems arise, answer the call. Rush to the scene to make a difference and keep your vision alive. You're not sure what to do? Don't worry about that. Just get out and lead. The mere fact that you're there, standing tall, will cause people to flock to you with ideas and resources.

All great leaders were baptized in fire and you'll be no exception.

FIRST MOVE—DO THIS NOW!

You know that one client for whom you are struggling to produce results? Maybe the problem is on your client's side. It could be that your team is failing your client. This is your chance to lead. Whether the problem is on your side or your client's, call a meeting with your team with the outcome of developing a plan to improve your results. Then call a meeting with your client to share the plan to improve those results. Then spend time with your client's team to help them make the changes necessary on their side. You must lead even when you do not have the formal authority.

RECOMMENDED READING

Arbinger Institute. *Leadership and Self-Deception: Getting Out of the Box*. San Francisco: Berrett-Koehler Publishers, 2002.

Roberts, Wess. *Leadership Secrets of Attila the Hun*. New York: Grand Central Publishing, 2007.

Sinek, Simon. *Start with Why: How Great Leaders Inspire Everyone to Take Action*. New York: Portfolio, 2011.

Chapter 19

EXERCISING THE SKILL-SET ELEMENTS TO CREATE A COMPETITIVE ADVANTAGE

Your product, company, brand, even your price are all table stakes. Ultimately, the most sustainable differentiation is the value you create in your customer's buying journey.

—Dave Brock, CEO of Partners in EXCELLENCE

THE GREAT GAME OF SALES HAS CHANGED—AND IT'S GOING TO keep changing. This isn't your daddy's sales game (or my mother's, for that matter). It's a very different world we live in, and that world includes a much tougher sales environment.

There are dozens of major forces and trends at work, all of which make selling more difficult, and all of which put downward pressure on margins (or profit). Let me introduce you to some of them.

Globalization has made the world smaller. In the United States, we were fine with outsourcing blue-collar work to countries such as China and India. But then we discovered that the Chinese and Indian people were every bit as sharp, every bit as savvy, and every bit as entrepreneurial as we are in the United States. You and your customers now have global competitors. This makes for greater competition and even more pressure on margins. This is one of the reasons that price dominates so many of your conversations with your dream clients.

If globalization isn't change enough, add to it disintermediation, another force that is radically reshaping the economic landscape. Disintermediation is a fancy way of saying "cut out the middle man." Amazon .com doesn't believe that you need to go to a bookstore to buy your books—or anything else, for that matter. It doesn't believe you need to go to Walmart; Amazon can ship you what you need. YouTube doesn't believe that you need television in its existing form, and it believes that everyone should have access to the tools that allow him to share his art, his political opinion, or whatever he believes entertains, informs, or persuades. Newspapers in their traditional form are dying, and so are many book publishers, record companies, television stations, and wholesalers. Read: more downward pressure on margins.

We had a deep recession in the United States when the dot-com bubble burst at the beginning of the twenty-first century. We ended the century's first decade with another significant downturn when the financial industry collapsed as a result of bad business practices, mostly around home mortgages. Led by the United States, the entire world was driven into the Great Recession. This has created what I earlier called "post-recessionary stress disorder." Even though the US economy faced only one year of negative growth (i.e., a shrinking economy), people still feel as if we might at any moment slip into another recession. This creates more fear and more pressure on margins as many people hold back from investing in their businesses because they believe the bottom could fall out at any minute. Still more pressure on price.

But wait . . . there's more.

The purchasing function in many businesses has grown stronger, and professional buyers continually look for ways to cut costs to increase their companies' profitability.

Companies are consolidating vendors in an attempt to capture volume discounts and drive down the costs of doing business with multiple suppliers.

Individuals at every level inside companies are now accountable for their lines on their firms' profit-and-loss reports—including low-level managers and supervisors who may never even have seen a P&L.

The Internet has, for many salespeople, created information parity. Buyers can do more research to understand with whom they might want to do business—and how much they might have to pay. (If your dream clients have information parity with you, you need to go back over the chapter on business acumen. Information parity is the fast track to a lack of value creation.)

All these factors lead to one giant result for salespeople: many of your prospective clients want to commoditize you and your offering. Many of them believe that you are no different from your competitors, and they believe that you cannot—or will not—create greater value.

This trend is tearing the world of sales in two.

WHY YOU MUST BE DIFFERENT

The world of sales is splitting into two branches: the consultative and the transactional. There is so much pressure to perform financially that many sales organizations are themselves becoming more transactional. These companies are focused on reducing their overall costs and automating much of what they do when it comes to sales, such as allowing their customers to learn about their offering online and to place orders there. They are also moving their sales forces from the field to inside sales roles, which pay less than field sales positions do.

Salespeople who can't or don't—or won't—create greater value for their dream clients and the companies they work for are going to get forced to the transactional side of a chasm that is just beginning to open (but widening all the time). However, there is another side of that chasm for those willing to leap across.

Sales organizations with complex, greater value-creating solutions are focused on solving their clients' most strategic challenges, spending time consulting with their dream clients, and differentiating their value propositions. Some of these companies may be moving the transactional sales to inside salespeople, but they are increasingly hiring more—and paying more for—salespeople who can develop relationships. This creates a higher level of value and differentiates these companies and their offerings.

As the gap in the world of sales widens, you'll have to choose which side to stand on. Developing the seventeen elements—the mind-set and the skill set of sales success—will help you leap from transactional to consultative sales. Don't take that as permission to become satisfied or lazy, though. You will have to keep working at those elements—and working on yourself.

YOU MUST DEVELOP YOURSELF PERSONALLY AND PROFESSIONALLY

There was a short period of time when companies felt obligated to develop their people personally and professionally. During this period (maybe from the 1950s through the late 1990s), companies also had the profit with which to make those investments. Though organizations *should* be investing more in developing people—as all the factors we've talked about in this chapter indicate—such investments are growing increasingly rare. There is too much drive for quarterly results, too much focus on shareholder value.

You don't have to like or agree with the fact that many companies don't invest enough in developing their people. You may feel very strongly that they have some duty to develop the folks they hire, and you may even wish that someone would spend more time and money helping you grow. But we are at the end of this book, and you know that you will find no quarter for those sentiments here.

It is 100 percent your responsibility to grow, to develop yourself both personally and professionally.

At the beginning of the book, I told you that the single difference between salespeople who perform at the highest level and those who lag behind isn't situational. It isn't their products, their service, their manager, or their compensation structure.

Instead, I said that success is individual. You have the power to make the call instead of avoiding it. You create value for your dream client, and you capture some of that value for your company.

Put simply, *you* are the difference that makes the difference.

By developing the mind-set elements in the first half of this book, you will differentiate yourself from the many salespeople with whom you compete. Very few of them will have your discipline, meaning that they will not be able to outwork you. Most won't have your positive attitude; instead, they'll look for excuses. They won't care as deeply, compete as ferociously, or be as resourceful. Your initiative, your determination, your ability to communicate, and your willingness to be accountable for results will make you the rarest of rare commodities. You will have influence beyond your peers, because you will be someone worth following.

By developing the skill-set elements in the second half of this book, you will make a bigger difference for your dream clients right from jump street. Your ability to ask for the commitments you need will allow you to help your dream clients in ways that your competitors can't imagine. Your message will be sharper when you are prospecting, and your stories will be more compelling. Your skill in diagnosing your dream clients' challenges will demonstrate that you have the business acumen to help, and discovering the ground truth will allow you to build consensus. Even though you may not have the title "leader," you'll leave no doubt as to who will ensure that the outcomes you've sold are obtained.

You've worked your way through the seventeen elements of sales success. You're better prepared to be the value creator that your dream client needs right now. But your work has just begun. You can never stop developing yourself personally and professionally. In this disruptive age, you need to continually sharpen your saw.

When you need a refresher, grab this book again. I recommend you flip through the book and your notes every quarter. Pick a chapter about a subject in which you feel you need some help. Go back over the work you've done as you've worked through the chapters of this book. Read one of the books listed at the end of that chapter.

And come and visit me at www.iannarino.com. I'll always have something new waiting for you there when you need it.

Go and be the difference that makes a difference. And do good work.

LAST MOVE—DO THIS NOW!

If you haven't already done so, go to www.theonlysalesguide.com and download the workbook that accompanies this book. Choose the one chapter that you really need to work on now, and complete all the exercises in that chapter. Once you have mastered that area of sales success, choose another chapter, and repeat until you've completed the whole workbook.

RECOMMENDED READING

McKain, Scott. *Collapse of Distinction: Stand out and Move up While Your Competition Fails.* Nashville, TN: Thomas Nelson, 2010.

Neumeier, Marty. *Zag: The Number-One Strategy of High-Performance Brands: A Whiteboard Overview.* Berkeley, CA: AIGA, 2007.

Trout, Jack. *Differentiate or Die: Survival in Our Era of Killer Competition.* Hoboken, NJ: Wiley, 2010.

ACKNOWLEDGMENTS, WITH GRATITUDE

A book like this requires a lot more than a mere acknowledgment of all the people who have shaped my thinking and helped me to produce it.

Writing a book is time-consuming. I am most grateful to my wife, Cher, for her constant support. Aidan, Mia, and Ava, my three children, have taught me more than I have taught them. I am proud and grateful for the people that they are becoming. My family would be unhappy if I didn't acknowledge Skamp, Chelsea, and Weird Henry, our two little Maltese dogs and our rescued cat.

Much of what I know I learned from my mother. She gets her own line here, and there has never been a better example of love in action. Whatever good qualities I may, from time to time, possess are her doing. Whatever shortcomings I have are my own, and they are certainly things she is still diligently working to correct.

I've also learned from two of the best salespeople you will ever encounter: my sisters, Thada Larmier (the best pure relationship builder you will ever meet) and Tara Iannarino (no one is more effective at prospecting anywhere on earth). My younger brother, Jason Iannarino, is a professional comedian. He has helped me with more than a line or two when something needed to be "punched up." My older brother, Mike, was instrumental in my development as a salesperson, riding shotgun when "selling" meant booking gigs for our band, Bad Reputation! We're still writing songs together!

My dad was an old-school salesperson. He closed on the first visit or lost the deal. He took me into homes in bad neighborhoods, where he enrolled kids in technical school and changed their lives. He was a great sales manager and a constant source of advice. He is also the reason I can speak in public.

My gratitude for my family at Solutions Staffing is immense. Peg Mativi has been a second mother to me. Much of what I know I learned from her, especially the law of putting profits above revenue (a lesson that could benefit many). Geoff Fullen is my partner in crime. We have worked together since we were kids, making messes, making mistakes, and building a great company together. He has taught me a great deal, and we are brothers until the end. Brandy Thompson, Amy Englert, Becky Kukay, Ron Zinko, Matt Woodland, Kelly Stinedurf, and the rest of the Solutions Staffing team are the best in the world at what they do, and I'd put them up against any team, anytime, anywhere.

Mary Vinnedge, my editor at *SUCCESS Magazine*, was instrumental in getting this book in shape for publication. Barry Fox was immensely helpful in tightening up my language and working through the developmental edits. Ted Kinni gave me direction on how best to lay out the book and helped me part with four elements, something that immeasurably improved the book.

I am grateful for Beth Mastre, Heather May, Bryan Thomas, Matt Steele, Casey Bobb-Etter, David Speakman, Steve Byrne, Malcolm Hingley, Mike Sheridan, Ricky Arriola, Jason Schlenker, Andrew and Nicole Honey of ThinkSales, Amy McTobin, and my friends at Kinopicz: Francesco, Damian, Amber, and Dave.

How can I go without showing the proper appreciation for my tribe? Special thanks to Mike Weinberg, Mark Hunter, Miles Austin, Jeb Blount, John Spence, Mike Kunkle, Leann Hoagland Smith, Matt Heinz, Lori Richardson, Doug Rice, Paul McCord, Tibor Shanto, Alen Mayer, Bob

Terson, Karin Bellantoni, Kelley Robertson, Todd Schnick, Alice R. Heiman, Gary Hart, Nancy Nardin, Andy Paul, Steven Rosen, Elinor Stutz, Richard Ruff and Janet Spirer, Dianna Gearin, Deb Calvert, Jack Malcolm, Jeff Beals, Jim Keenan, Babbette Ten Haken, Dan Waldschmidt, Tim Ohai, Kelly Riggs, Dorian Lynn Hidy, Doyle Slayton, and Kelly Mc-Cormick.

I must also thank some unofficial tribe members and mentors, including the world's foremost authority on trust, Charlie Green; the man who taught me most of what I know about using the social tools, my brother, Chris Brogan; the person I turn to when I need advice on sales leadership, the brilliant Dave Brock; and the person who has given me hours of her time explaining the writing and speaking business, Jill Konrath. Bob Burg is a great friend and someone who is always willing to lend a hand when I need one. And I am grateful to the inimitable Gerhard Gschwandtner, my Austrian brother.

INDEX

INDEX

MONEY-BACK GUARANTEE

If you apply the principles in this book faithfully for the next ninety days, your sales results will improve significantly—I guarantee it.

If you don't see an increase in your sales by at least 10 percent within three months, send a letter outlining your sales work and proof of purchase to me at the address below and I'll refund the original price of your book.

ANTHONY IANNARINO
c/o Portfolio / Penguin
An imprint of Penguin Random House LLC
375 Hudson Street
New York, N.Y. 10014
U.S.A.

Need more? For a practical, groundbreaking new approach to closing the deal, don't miss *The Lost Art of Closing*

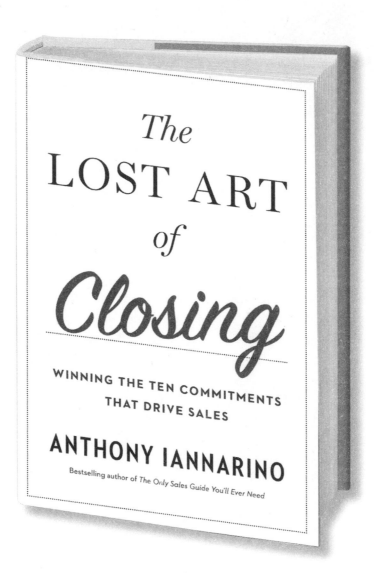

www.TheSalesBlog.com